SIOBHÁN: A MEMOIR OF AN ACTRESS

Do Nuala, a chabhraig leis an taighde.

Siobhán

A Memoir of an Actress

Micheál Ó hAodha

BRANDON

First published in 1994 by
Brandon Book Publishers Ltd
Dingle, Co. Kerry, Ireland

British Library Cataloguing in Publication Data
is available for this book.

ISBN 0 86322 188 2

This book is published with the financial assistance of
the Arts Council/An Chomhairle Ealaíon, Ireland.

Photo credits: Plates 1 and 2 reproduced with permission
from The Irish Times; Plate 5 reproduced with permission
from the Dublin Gate Theatre; Plate 6 Cecil Beaton
photograph courtesy of Sotheby's, London; Plate 7 reproduced with permission from The Kerryman; Plate 10
reproduced with permission from the Druid Theatre
Company, Galway, and Amelia Stein; Plate 11 reproduced by permission of John Hippisley.

Cover design by The Graphiconies, Dublin
Typeset by Koinonia Ltd, Bury
Printed by Redwood Books, Wilts

Contents

List of Illustrations

Acknowledgements

It was my friend Riobárd MacGóráin of Gael-Linn who first suggested to me a biography in Irish of Siobhán McKenna, but, regrettably, I found it impossible to complete that work. This memoir could not have been written without the generous co-operation of Siobhán's son, Donnacha O'Dea, who gave me access to her correspondence and papers, provided photographs and answered my many questions about her life. Her sister, Nancy McMahon, and her cousin Sister Benevenuta OP (Dr Margaret MacCurtain of University College, Dublin) were particularly helpful in piecing together Siobhán's family background and details of her public career.

I owe a particular debt of gratitude to Johnny Hippisley of Quest Productions, Niall Buggy, and Tomás MacAnna of the Abbey Theatre who wrote or recorded personal reminiscences of Siobhán. Michael Johnston kindly made available to me extracts from an unpublished biography of his mother Shelah Richards, compiled by Robert Hogan from notes and recordings made by her in 1982/83.

All the following have helped, answering correspondance or allowing me to interview them: the late Cyril Cusack, Conor Cruise O'Brien, Ulick O'Connor, Lelia Doolan, Joe Dowling, Brian McGrath, Graham Sheperd, Tomás Hardiman, Art O'Briain, Pádraic O'Farrell, Maelíosa Stafford, Jane Daly, Deirdre McQuillan, Mary

Murphy, Alan Brien, Christopher Fitz-Simon, Betsy Nealan, Eileen Brosnan, Michael Travers, Bridie Foley, Kate Ashe, Dan Foley, Seumas MacConville, Martin Whelan and Padraic Ó Raghallaigh. Mary Corcoran and RTE, Mary Clark of the Dublin Corporation Theatre Archive, Michael Costello of the Kerry County Library and Kathleen Hackett who filed Siobhán's papers, all proved very helpful, as were Becky O'Connor who typed the manuscript, and Peter Malone and Steve MacDonogh of Brandon Book Publishers. The newspapers, magazines and periodicals quoted are acknowledged in the notes.

Micheál Ó hAodha
August, 1994

Bird's Nest

WHEN SIOBHÁN MCKENNA was laid to rest in Rahoon on 18 November 1986, the rain was not falling softly, softly falling, but pouring down pitilessly on the living and the dead. It was the graveyard where Nora Barnacle's first lovers, Michael Feeney and Sonny Bodkin, had been buried and James Joyce had written of Nora weeping over Rahoon:

> Rain in Rahoon falls softly, softly falling,
> Where my dark love lies,
> Sad is his voice that calls me, sadly calling
> At grey moonrise.
>
> Love hear thou
> How soft, how sad his voice is ever calling,
> Ever unanswered, and the dark rain falling,
> Then as now.
>
> Dark too our hearts, O love, shall lie and cold
> As his sad heart has lain
> Under the moongrey nettles, the black mould
> And muttering rain.[1]

Nora Barnacle's Rahoon was out in the country, over two miles from the centre of old Galway. Today, the cemetery is surrounded by

9

a suburban sprawl, a housing estate whose residents in their violent resistance to the settlement of travellers there gave currency to a new word – "Rahoonery". A new Siobhán McKenna Road between Shantalla and Rahoon may yet efface that memory.

Siobhán's old friends and neighbours, drenched to the skin in Rahoon, reminded one another that happy is the corpse that the rain pours on. The old Connemara women spoke of *Samhain* (November) as the month of falling stars, said to be souls on their way to paradise. Hundreds of mourners craned their necks for a glimpse of the coffin, beneath a hillock of flowers, the only brightness in a pool of desolation.

After the prayers in Irish and a lament by a lone piper, Brian Friel, most distinguished of playwrights and most taciturn of men, spoke movingly in a short funeral oration of Siobhán's "star quality, her stage presence and her humanity and generosity". Siobhán had made "the idea of Ireland she personified seem almost possible".

In the future, the younger generation will probably shrug their shoulders when people say, "But you should have seen Siobhán McKenna as Saint Joan, or Pegeen Mike or Cass Maguire," but they will not know and little will be left to tell them – some reels of cinema and television film – what she was really like. She will perhaps live on, as a legend, but the stage actor's work dies almost wholly with the performer.

When Siobhán died of cardiac arrest at the Blackrock Clinic, Dublin, on 16 November 1986, after two operations for lung cancer, a Dublin journalist wrote that like Edmund Kean she had played her great parts "as 'twere by flashes of lightning". Others recalled that, like Othello, she had done the state some service, having being chosen by the President of Ireland, Cearbhall Ó Dálaigh, in 1976, as the first artist ever to serve on the Council of State. But her public life, in which she did not shun controversy, was not her real self. Her private life, as a lover, a wife, a mother and a companion of infinite gaiety, was a storehouse of memories. In her early years she was a brilliant student, the translator into Irish of Shaw, J.M. Barrie and other playwrights. Her real life, though, was spent on the boards acting, and rehearsing when she was not acting. She was essentially a stage actress who won international fame without ever compromising her quintessential Irishness. On the day after she died, Ulick O'Connor recalled:

When Siobhán McKenna came on the stage, you knew what it must have been like to watch Sarah Bernhardt, Ellen Terry or Eleanora Duse. She was our only *grande dame*. The atmosphere was electric; her eyes would sweep the audience like a searchlight. Her voice had a distinct pitch which compelled attention and the light would catch her high cheekbones to sculpt the rest of the face.

People just referred to her as Siobhán – just as they did with Sarah, Ellen or Eleanora.... Whenever there was an argument as to whether or not an Abbey style of acting existed, you had only to point to Siobhán and Cyril Cusack. Now Cyril must carry the flame kindled in those golden years when our national theatre made its name notable in the theatrical history of this century.[2]

She was born in Saint James's Park, off the Falls Road, Belfast, on 24 May 1922, the second daughter of Eoin McKenna, a teacher of mathematics in a technical school and an extra-mural lecturer in Queen's University. A studious and scholarly Corkman, he had earlier held teaching posts at the Presentation College, Cork, at St Colman's, Fermoy, and for a short time at Greenock in Scotland. As an extern student of London University, he took an MA degree in mathematics. Before coming to Belfast he had married Margaret ("Gretta") O'Reilly from Granard, Co. Longford, a fashion buyer in the drapery trade and a very successful businesswoman whose family did not think that she had made "a good match". Teaching was a poorly paid profession in the early twenties.

Although born in the years of the establishment of partition and the Belfast pogroms, Siobhán's earliest memories of the city were of the shipyard sirens, unecumenical church bells, and the animated voices of the factory girls.

There was no acting tradition on either side of her family, but there was an acceptance of play-acting as fun. What her father took seriously was his own discipline, mathematics, and he had an abiding love of the Irish language, no matter where his professional career took him. Siobhán's mother attended Gaelic League classes in Belfast, but it was not until Siobhán Ní Mhainín, a native speaker from Ballyferriter, Co. Kerry, came as a housekeeper that the McKennas became an Irish-speaking family. Siobhán recalled later that her father would read *Jimín Mháire Thaidhg* at bedtime and that An Seabhac's hilarious account of a Kerry gorsoon provided laughter in a new language. Her memories of her first home in Saint James's Park were blurred by a move to Clonard Gardens beside the Roman Catholic church. When she was three-and-a-half years of age she was sent with her only sister, Nancy, eighteen months her senior, to a Montessori school run by the Dominican nuns on the Falls Road. It was a child's world of plasticine, raffia and rosary beads, remote from any rumble of an orange drum or a verse of "The Sash". The only drama was provided by the older and "wilder" Nancy, who was specially dressed by her mother in a green costume with Celtic embroidery for a recitation at a school concert. According to the elocution teacher, Mother Pius, Nancy had a wonderful voice while Siobhán had a Belfast accent, which later helped her to get her first important part at the Abbey Theatre in Joseph Tomelty's *The End House*. During school years Siobhán always saw Nancy as the tragedienne, while she felt more suited to comic roles. Over forty years later Siobhán wrote of her childhood:

> Clonard was a village, really. I remember a bookshop where my father used to take me. It was small, with books right up to the ceiling. There was a double-ladder, on top of which they would let me sit, and I'd take great delight in surveying the different-coloured backs. There was another man who must have had a toffee factory because he'd bring us large slabs of it which you literally broke with a hammer.
>
> I remember being taken into the city for a special treat. One was *Cinderella* at the Opera House. It was all white and silver with real white ponies on the stage, the coach a mass of sparkling diamonds. The pumpkin disappeared under my very nose. The ballroom scene was all white. It was so indescribably beautiful. Never have I seen anything so magical except for the countryside itself when covered in the first untrodden fall of snow. We were sitting away up top, but it could not have been at the very top because balloons were released from further up at the interval and I got two.[3]

Her mother was deeply religious and when her father got the post of lecturer in mathematics at University College Galway it was attributed to the power of prayer. They did not leave Belfast until Siobhán had made her first holy communion in May 1927. Her account of her first confession has something of the fanciful charm of Frank O'Connor's famous short story:

For confession she [Sister Paula] stressed that I must only tell the important sins and not waste the priest's time. I could not think of any except when my father would ask my sister to jump into his arms, whereas I wouldn't budge and say "I want my mammy." I decided this was not a big enough sin. That morning, having also being warned to speak up, I told the priest in a loud voice that I'd stolen £100 from my mother's pocket. He said, "Three Hail Mary's, child." My mother explained to me afterwards that the sins had to be true and that God help me she hadn't got as much as a hundred pence for anyone to steal.[4]

It was an accidental rendezvous with a corpse that awoke in Siobhán a sense of make-believe and drama. One day Siobhán and some other children were told that a man in the neighbourhood had died and that there would be cake and lemonade for anybody who went to see him "laid out". They decided it was too good to miss.

You entered the kitchen-cum-living room from the street. There was a staircase as you went in the door. A woman in a chair just by it. She had a funny smile on her face. Her husband was in an open coffin resting on two chairs. He was like yellow marble except for his stiff moustache.

We knelt down to pray. Then we were given a piece of cake each and a cup of lemonade. As we munched, I could not take my eyes off the woman near the stairs and I whispered to my girlfriend that she must have poisoned him. Next day there were rumours flying but my mother soon scotched them and gave me a prim talking to, explaining that a nervous twitch could not be mistaken for a smile. That evening I practised a nervous twitch in my mother's mirror. I began to imagine what it would be like if my mother were to be taken away. I dissolved into tears.

Nevertheless, wakes still continued to fascinate me and soon I led a small army upstairs this time. The poor man must have died in his sleep for he was sitting bolt upright with his brown eyes glaring at me. I turned tail without a prayer, shouting "He's alive. He's alive." The poor wife came rushing down but we didn't stop for cake. The incident put me off brown eyes for some time.[5]

On the day of their departure, Siobhán felt lonely for the little streets of Belfast, where she had played hopscotch on the chalked pavements. Galway, however, was a splendid backdrop for the actress-to-be. Even the change of homes provided a bigger stage. The McKennas were installed in Fort Eyre in Shantalla, an old rambling mansion which had originally been built by Cromwell's commander-in-chief, James Edges Eyre, who gave his name to the square in the city's centre. There was a stone tower on the grounds, named the Penny Tower, as labourers were paid a penny a day to build it. The oldest portion of the present house had been built in about 1800 but in the early years of this century it was divided into several units, one of which was named Hansberry House, and it was here that the McKennas lived. Shantalla was then on the edge of the countryside and for Siobhán, "It was love at first sight, for the four of us, my mother, father, Nancy and I."

Salthill was beautifully wild then. The canals were smooth flowing, the Corrib sometimes tumbling wildly under all these bridges and the town-clock in Saint Nicholas', which my mother could read even if it was two miles away, and above all, the people. I think there must be something in the air of the West which is wild and untameable and soaring. From the very first night in Galway, I always remember that sensation of wanting to fly and I developed a passion for climbing trees to the topmost branch, much to my mother's concern. The placid child now flew everywhere. Icarus wasn't in it. Wild asses held no fear for me: flying down the hill perched on one pedal of my father's bike and eventually mastering the intricate art of cycling with one leg under the bar.[6]

Siobhán, however, was not allowed to grow up an unladylike Mad Sweeney among the trees. Again she found herself in the care of the Dominican nuns, this time at their fashionable convent school on Taylor's Hill. On her first morning she was asked to recite for the class. She chose:

I met a little elfman once
Down where the lilies blow
I asked him why he was so small
And why he did not grow.
At first he looked me up and down
Then looked me through and through
I am as big for me he said
As you are big for you.

14

The entire class rocked with laughter and Siobhán thought she was an enormous success, with her sister Nancy's gift for recitation. Soon she was dismayed on learning that they were really amused at her strange Belfast accent, which sounded like water gurgling from a bottle. She was soon to become familiar with other accents and other places.

Siobhán Ní Mhainín brought me to stay with her in Ballyferriter one summer. My chief pleasure was collecting the eggs for her mother. I didn't know why the hens kept sitting on their eggs, so I'd shoo them off. One day an unfortunate hen had to take rapid flight and, to my astonishment, I saw a white object coming out from under her tail. I didn't eat eggs for years afterwards. Most holidays were with my grandmother on the shores of Loch Gamhna in County Longford. My Dublin cousins came, too: May and Peggy and Sheila.

I remember the mystery of the plantation, the woods, streams and the lake; wild raspberries in profusion and billberries which turned our mouths purple. Fr. Plunkett was a relation and he'd arrive on a high horse-trap with baskets of rosy apples. He was old but he had rosy cheeks. I used to wonder if there was any connection between the two. Christmas morning in Colmcille Chapel was lit only by candles and storm-lanterns. The postman delivered letters and parcels on that day. I remember him walking in a peculiar fashion. When he was leaving my uncle took his arm to accompany him to the next townland.[7]

Without knowing it, Siobhán had taken one of her first acting lessons in her simple observation of country life and the gait of a tipsy postman. She seemed to possess a photographic memory of all the people she had met and the places she had seen. She once freakishly described herself as a calf with four legs, with a leg in each province – she claimed relationship with Royal Meath through the O'Reillys – but her firmest leg was now rooted in Galway and the west. With the encouragement of Eoin McKenna, Siobhán Ní Mhainín had gone to night classes, matriculated, and won a scholarship to University College Galway. She was replaced as a housekeeper by a girl from near Spiddal, so Siobhán's ear became quickly attuned to the idioms of Connacht Irish. The new girl, Nan, was nicknamed "the gramophone" by the neighbours as she always went about her business singing *sean-nós* or traditional songs. She was so mad for dancing sets at Rahoon crossroads that she wore out a pair

15

of shoes each month. On a Monday morning, Siobhán often heard
her sing like a wounded blackbird:

Tá pian i mbéal mo cleibhe
Do chuirfeadh na céadta fear chun bháis.
[I have a pain in my gullet
would slay hundreds of fellas.]

Another wing of Fort Eyre was occupied by Seán Mac Giollar-
náth, a district justice with splendid Irish, in which he wrote several
books on the fauna and flora of Connemara. He had a large garden
and gave Siobhán and her friends their first lessons in nature study.
They learned more than the DJ intended:

We kids discovered something else went on down the Red Lane –
lovers' nests built into the bushes. We'd arm ourselves with a can
of water and bicycle pumps, fill the pumps and squirt the water
through the branches at the lovers, then fly off squeaking with
delight and terror with the lovers in hot pursuit.[8]

Soon there were *céilí* dances to the music of a blind piper, and a
seanchaí with stories of the headless coachman who stopped "every
night, once a month, twice a year" outside Fort Eyre. As might be
expected, Siobhán heard the rattle of the wheels every night from
then on as fears which the folktale aroused conflicted with an interest
in the lovers' nests in the bushes. Her imagination was now afire,
not for the theatre, which was virtually unknown to her, but for
play-acting. She and Nancy concocted the most lurid of melodramas
which they staged in McNally's barn, and all the neighbouring
children would gather to see the pair. Nancy of the flame-red hair
was always the lovesick heroine and Siobhán the dyed-in-the-wool
villain with glued-on mattress-hair for a moustache.

Siobhán got swollen glands, usually a symptom of primary tuber-
culosis, a serious illness in those years, generally ignored by poorer
families, with often fatal results. Siobhán was confined to bed for
nearly a year, during which she read Dickens and Thomas Hardy.
She recovered fully, convinced that Galway could never be like
Wessex, and her only complaint about her enforced leisure was that
she had put on weight and was called "Fatty" by her schoolmates.

When I was allowed my first walk, my mother took me up the
road to Rahoon... I was now amazed at the beauty I saw all over

again. I kept exclaiming at the beauty of the sky or a cloud or a calf or a lamb or a daisy or a celandine as I walked slowly along. Although I was still very young, I grew up that day and understood somewhere inside that life was a miracle, something to be enjoyed and marvelled at always, and the Galway sky which is higher than any other sky was higher than ever.[9]

She always spoke and wrote of her schooldays with warmth and charm. She was spirited, stubborn and liked to act the tomboy. Convent girls were not allowed to take part in the rumpus and ructions which were part of the annual rag-day at University College, which included throwing flour on innocent or inquisitive bystanders as part of the disorderly rampage through the streets and suburbs. Because one of the nuns had suffered this indignity there was a convent rule that no student should attend the rag. Siobhán and some others asked for the ban to be removed. When the Mother Superior refused, Siobhán broke bounds and went outside the convent gates to witness the student pranks. One neurotic nun was so shocked by Siobhán's behaviour that she doused her with holy water to exorcise such high spirits and then had her expelled from the school.

Siobhán dreaded her father's anger, but he viewed his daughter's misbehaviour with academic calm. In the autumn of 1936 he sent Siobhán as a boarder to the St Louis Convent, Monaghan, a highly respected secondary school where most subjects were taught through Irish.

Mother Lorcán (Stuart), a friend of her father, took a special interest in Siobhán's progress. Although she was an indifferent singer, she played principal parts in the school operettas, mainly Gilbert and Sullivan, an exotic hybrid in an "A" or All-Irish school. Every class produced a play and Siobhán chose to produce and play the name part of *Charley's Aunt*. She was probably the only female ever to play this double role as the copyright holders insisted that no actress should ever appear in the part.

After one of the school productions, she was asked to say a few words of thanks to a distinguished visitor, the writer Sir Shane Leslie. She did so graciously, but as she backed away bowing, she put her seat on the keyboard of an open piano. Sir Shane complimented her on having at last discovered the Lost Chord, with apologies to Groucho Marx.

Of course, there were studies as well. Siobhán had her father's gift for mathematics and a good ear for French, but elocution and physical culture, as it was then called, bored her. Lessons in etiquette reduced her to helpless giggles which infected the whole class. She did not realise that the stilted elocution lessons and the poker-backed deportment demonstrations, then a source of fun to her, were teaching her how to look perfectly serious while acting the fool. Her talent for making people laugh won her admirers even among the sternest of the religious sisters. During her years in Monaghan, success at her studies was uppermost in her mind and she left with an honours Leaving Certificate and a scholarship to University College Galway. Over forty years later, the St Louis Convent would proudly show to visitors a collection of theatrical memorabilia of the school's most celebrated pupil.

Siobhán's move from the cloistered life at Monaghan, where she fantasised about taking the veil, to the equivocal atmosphere of the conventionally Catholic Galway university was hardly traumatic. It was still a sexually divided institution in which students "did lines" but did not cohabit. The love ditties of her boyfriends were as innocent as those of a Christmas cracker:

> I would that I were Santa Claus
> (Ó Broin will think this shockin')
> 'Cos I'd like to come and leave
> A ladder in yer stockin'.

All academic, social and club activities were strictly supervised by the president, Monsignor "Pa" Hynes, who in turn was supervised by the Most Reverend Michael Browne, Bishop of Galway. Siobhán's father was now Professor of Mathematical Physics and an ardent supporter of Gaelic games. All subjects at the university, except English, were taught through Irish and Siobhán attended her father's classes for mathematics and those of Professor Liam Ó Briain for French. After her years in Monaghan, she had a trim athletic figure and became captain of the university camogie team. Irish was more than ever the home language. The "gramophone" Nan had left to get married and was replaced by Máire Nic Giolla Mhairtín, a native speaker from Connemara with considerable talent as an amateur actress.

From as early as she could remember, Siobhán had attended the

Christmas pantomimes at An Taibhdhearc, the Irish-speaking theatre which had been founded in 1928 by Micheál MacLiammóir and Hilton Edwards with the benefit of a small annual subsidy from the government. She had also seen Anew McMaster and Company who toured the length and breadth of the country in the thirties and forties, playing mainly Shakespeare. The semi-professional company at An Taibhdhearc depended largely on student talent from the university and on army personnel from the Irish-speaking battalion at Renmore Barracks. Although her academic career was uppermost in her mind, it seemed inevitable that sooner or later Siobhán would be invited to play at An Taibhdhearc. She was fortunate that her French professor, Liam Ó Briain, was a founding director of An Taibhdhearc: it was he who had persuaded MacLiammóir and Edwards many years earlier to come to Galway. He recommended her to the resident producer and leading actor, Walter (Wally) Macken. To keep the little theatre alive, Macken had also to work as scene painter, stage designer and playwright. He slept and lived in the theatre. He trained the raw recruits from Renmore and the boisterous undergraduates from the university by throwing them in at the deep end where they would either act or sink. The more sophisticated Siobhán was offered a playing salary of thirty shillings a week, but her father would not allow her to accept it, saying that she should be glad of the opportunity to improve her Irish.

Macken, who had such a fruitful influence on Siobhán's apprenticeship, had not her privileged background. He had to struggle from modest beginnings to make a career for himself in the theatre. His father, a carpenter who had acted in the old Rackets Court Theatre in Middle Street, Galway, joined the British Army and was killed in the trenches in France in March 1916, when his youngest son Walter was only ten months old. After he left primary school, Walter joined the Taibhdhearc Theatre, where he showed such all-round ability that he was appointed manager in 1939. As well as acting and playwriting at An Taibhdhearc and later at the Abbey Theatre he also gained a considerable reputation as a novelist. The success of his third novel *Rain on the Wind* in 1950 made it possible for him to return to live in Connemara as a full-time writer of novels, plays and short stories, but he never returned to An Taibhdhearc which he had served so selflessly and so splendidly.

Siobhán's first appearance was in a pageant about St Patrick in which she played one of the pagan daughters of the High King of

Tara. After a deathbed conversion she was baptised and miraculously died on the spot. Siobhán giggled through her death throes, but the cast and audience said that they never saw such a moving death scene. Walter Macken said, "You died so gracefully."

If she considered herself an actress at all, it was as a comedienne. After a small part in Eugene O'Neill's *Emperor Jones* in 1941, she could not take Walter Macken seriously when he told her that he had cast her to play Lady Macbeth. But she did so intuitively, looking incongruously youthful with a round face and two long plaits. When Macken asked her to play in her own translation of J. M. Barrie's *Mary Rose*, she found it hard to believe in herself as a romantic heroine who was a stolen child of the fairy *sidhe*. Liam Ó Briain wanted her to play the lead in his own translation of *Le National Six*, by Jean Jacques Bernard, billed as *Ar an mBóthar Mór*. Shrewdly she told him that she was too busy studying to learn the part. He would not listen to her excuse.

"But will I get first-class honours in French?" coaxed Siobhán.

"You'll probably get second class," replied the professor gruffly.

As things turned out, she got first-class honours: despite her roles at An Taibhdhearc she had never thought of acting as a career and did not neglect her studies. She graduated with an honours BA in 1943, and with a scholarship to University College Dublin, where she enrolled for a masters degree in French under Professor Roger Chauviré. In digs in Leeson Park, she had hardly got down to serious study when she was invited to attend an audition at the Abbey Theatre. She did not take the offer too seriously and only went along when pressed to do so by her fellow students in the digs, a lively bunch according to Siobhán, "very like the girls in Edna O'Brien's early novels". But there can be little doubt that her former professor, Liam Ó Briain, a regular visitor to the Abbey, had told Ernest Blythe, the managing director of that theatre, that an actress of real potential had come to study in UCD.

That autocratic northerner, Blythe, who took command soon after the death of Yeats in 1939, had persuaded the Fianna Fáil government under Eamon de Valera that the grant previously paid to An Comhar Drámaíochta for the production of plays in Irish should be transferred to the Abbey for regular professional productions in that language. This plan had been fully implemented in 1941 and the former Taibhdhearc producer Proinsias Mac Diarmada (Frank Dermody) and some other actors from the Gaeltacht had joined the company. Blythe went further by encouraging even senior players like Denis O'Dea to spend some time in the Gaeltacht at the Abbey's expense, so as to improve their knowledge of the spoken language.

Still very much the professor's daughter with no consuming passion for the theatre, she was ill-prepared for the audition. In her haste to reach the theatre in time, she fell from her bicycle and arrived late with a skinned kneecap and muddy hands. Frank Dermody told her to pull herself together while Blythe wanted to know what she intended to perform.

"I will do anything you like," she replied diffidently, having no set piece prepared. Dermody suggested that she should go back to her digs to get scripts of *Mary Rose* and *Macbeth*.

After this long delay she told Blythe that she would like to play the scene between Mary Rose and her son, Simon. She asked if they could supply an actor to read the part of Simon but nobody was available.

"You will have to visualise him," said Blythe grumpily.

Siobhán simply put a chair on stage to represent Simon and only then realised that most of her own lines in the scene consisted of "*Sea*" and "*Ní hea*" (Yes and No).

"*Nach bhfuil aon spéic fada agat?*" demanded an exasperated Blythe who wanted to hear her in a longer piece of dialogue.

So Siobhán launched into the Irish version of Lady Macbeth's soliloquy:

Come to my woman's breasts
And take my milk for gall, you murd'ring ministers
Wherever in your slightest substances
You wait on nature's mischief! Come, thick night,
And pall thee in the dunnest smoke of hell!
That my keen knife see not the wound it makes
Nor heaven peep through the blanket of the dark,
To cry, *Hold, Hold!*

Blythe had heard enough and stopped her: "The Taibhdhearc is a bit broad. Too exaggerated for the Abbey. Can you type? You could maybe help out in the office in between parts in Irish plays."

Siobhán said she couldn't in between lectures at the university and studying for her MA. By now stage-hands and a few of the Abbey players had gathered to have a closer look at the daft one from Galway who did not seem to be afraid of Blythe. An Abbey droll, Dermot Kelly, told her later that whatever about Lady Macbeth, he liked her Mary Rose because he had never heard "Yes" and "No" said with such a variety of intonations.

Although he did not enthuse, Blythe gave her a contract. She was now what her father dreaded – a university drop-out and a fly-by-night actress at the Abbey. She was paid four pounds a week when playing and half-salary when resting (her mother would send eggs and brown bread), so she moved into a bedsitter in Northbrook Road. If she would never be a teacher or a writer, she was determined to be somebody. If she was going to be an actress, she would try to be the best. No easy task in the Abbey Theatre of the forties where newcomers, like well-behaved children, were supposed to be seen but not heard.

Everything went smoothly for Siobhán while she was playing in Irish language plays. So uneventful was her first appearance at the Abbey on 26 April 1944, in *Stiana*, a new play by the Gaelic League veteran, Peadar Ó hAnnracháin, that it seems to have escaped the notice of everybody including herself, for in later life she always claimed that her first appearance on the Abbey stage was in *Sodar i nDiaidh na nUasal*, a translation by Earnán de Blaghd (Ernest Blythe) of Molière's *Le Bourgeois Gentilhomme* in which she played Nicole, the maid, which was first produced on 21 May 1944. Her part required that she should laugh heartily and frequently at the antics of her master, Monsieur Jourdain. Now, the irrepressible giggler found it difficult to laugh aloud with conviction because she did not think the actor playing Jourdain very amusing. The producer, Frank Dermody, an impatient perfectionist, tried to help her but without success. Always resourceful, Siobhán consulted the original French text where to her delight the laughs were indicated as if in musical notation – há, há, há ... hé, hé, hé ... hó, hó, hó. Well after midnight, she would practise her laughing scales fortissimo in her bedsitter in Northbrook Road. After the other lodgers had complained of the strange noises, the landlady came to the door to enquire if Siobhán was as disturbed as she sounded. Only then, fearing that the landlady might try to have her seen by a doctor, did Siobhán admit that she was an actress at the Abbey, an occupation held in low esteem by flat-owners in those days. Much to her surprise, the landlady revealed that she liked the Abbey and gave

Siobhán a slight reduction in the rent of fifteen shillings a week.

One day Blythe came personally to ask Siobhán to go immediately to the Abbey to understudy one of the leading players, Eithne Dunne, who was losing her voice. Siobhán studied the moves of an actress she greatly admired and stayed up all night learning the lines. She arrived at the theatre next day to find that Eithne Dunne had recovered her voice. In another play in English, Joan Plunkett was feeling unwell and Siobhán was ready to take over, but Joan also recovered. It all seemed to prove MacLiammóir right when he quipped, "Get good understudies and none of the cast will go down sick."

Her first chance to play a part in English came on 21 August 1944, when she played a Belfast factory girl in Joseph Tomelty's *The End House*. In a cast which included F.J. McCormick, Cyril Cusack, Denis O'Dea, Eileen Crowe and May Craig, Siobhán received excellent notices as the spirited young woman who would not conform to the sectarian dictates of Orange or Green. She did not, however, wake up one morning in Northbrook Road to find herself famous; such pretensions were strickly frowned on in the Abbey of the forties. There were other young actresses in the company, like Eithne Dunne and Máire Ní Dhomhnaill, who had exceptional talent and experience. Siobhán had to prove herself in new plays, and in revivals she had to match the performances of earlier juvenile leads like Ria Mooney and Shelah Richards. Her fame would be built up laboriously, stone by stone.

Although she was working continuously, her salary had to be supplemented by an occasional present of a fiver from her father, who had become reconciled to the idea of a daughter who preferred comedy to calculus. Liam Ó Briain, of course, never lost faith in her. Frank Dermody was a sympathetic director and Ernest Blythe probably had a special *grá* for her because she was born in Belfast and spoke Irish.

There were some fortuitous circumstances which hastened Siobhán's emergence as one of the outstanding discoveries of the forties. Her arrival at the Abbey more or less coincided with one of those internal dissensions which seem to have beset the theatre's progress at various stages since its foundation in 1904. Although it had always been the policy of the theatre to produce plays in Irish, there had been only occasional productions in the language until Blythe was invited by Yeats to become a director. But Blythe's policy in the early forties of recruiting actors from the west for Irish-speaking parts and bringing in directors from An Taibhdhearc aroused understandable opposition from well-established players with no knowledge of the language.

Early in 1945 a group of dissenting players, including Liam Redmond, Gerard Healy and his wife Eithne Dunne, resigned from the Abbey to form a new company, The Players Theatre, for the production of what they considered more meritorious Irish plays than those staged at the Abbey. Their first production was Gerard Healy's *The Black Stranger*, a well-constructed play of the Famine times, which would have fitted nicely into the Abbey's usual stock of peasant drama. While the Abbey lost the work of a playwright of promise in Healy and a highly effective character actor in Liam Redmond, the departure of Eithne Dunne was a particularly severe blow. Understandably she wanted to play the leading role in her husband's play and she contributed greatly to its success at the Cork Opera House and later at the Gate Theatre in Dublin. Elated by this first triumph, The Players Theatre company booked the twelve-hundred-seater Olympia Theatre for a season of new Irish plays but failed to repeat the artistic or box-office success of *The Black Stranger*. The company disbanded and the leading actors left for film work in *I See a Dark Stranger*, one of the first successes of the post-war British cinema.

The harsh criticism directed at the Abbey at this time was extremely hurtful to Siobhán and other Irish speakers, although the departure of Eithne Dunne had virtually made her an automatic choice for most juvenile leads. She was proud to share a stage with most of the senior players who remained loyal to the Abbey, especially her idol F.J. McCormick, who had played all the great parts from Joxer to King Lear. One of the finest actors ever to play on a Dublin stage, he was virtually unknown outside Ireland except for occasional appearances with the Abbey company on tour in the United States. It happened that both F.J. and Siobhán were offered parts in *I See a Dark Stranger*. McCormick considered the part stage-Irish and refused. Siobhán, who was to play his daughter in the movie, consulted F.J., who said that she was a "natural" for the part but that if she really wanted to learn acting she should stay with the Abbey for at least three years. She decided to stay. McCormick's wife, Eileen Crowe, said dryly to Siobhán: "It's bad enough that he's a fool without making a fool of you also."

Siobhán played opposite McCormick in Shaw's two-hander, *Village Wooing,* and they got on famously together. She marvelled at F.J.'s power of infectious laughter. He did not make the sound of laughter; it was laughter in mime. His whole face puckered up and his shoulders shook in unison with the gales of laughter which came from the audience. She thought ruefully of her "ha-ha-has" and "he-he-hes" in the Molière play. Sometimes audiences over-reacted to McCormick's inventions and laughed in the wrong place. Whenever that happened, F.J. stopped in his tracks, stood absolutely still, and did not speak or move a muscle. Later he explained to Siobhán that audiences are like children: they get worried if you are doing nothing. Another of the great Abbey actors, M.J. Dolan, whom Siobhán admired, used the same technique.

Another of her favourites was May Craig, who had played Honor Blake in the original production of *The Playboy of the Western World* in 1907. When Siobhán saw her play the medium in *The Words Upon the Window Pane*, she knew what Yeats had meant when he had said: "When May Craig leaves her dressing room, she locks her door and leaves May Craig inside and becomes Mrs Henderson." Offstage, May Craig always wore wonderful picture hats and occasionally lent one to Siobhán for a part or a party. When Siobhán played the minor role of the woman from Rathmines in *The Plough and the Stars*, she lent her a fur coat and a hat with a long feather in it.

The Abbey actors lived in a different world from their colleagues at the Gate Theatre on Parnell Square. The Edwards and MacLiammóir company and Longford Productions were more mannered and colourful both on and off stage. If they did not all come from a sophisticated upper-class background, they sounded as if they did. The Abbey crowd were more down to earth and hail-fellow-well-met with ordinary Dubliners. You might meet the actors in a pub or a bookie's office and the actresses did not try to be glamorous. Siobhán was no exception. I was introduced to her at a "hop" in a popular dancehall on Adelaide Road. With her long tresses of reddish-brown hair, her greenish-brown eyes, puckish smile and freckled face, she was the lass with the delicate air. She looked not so much at you as through you, but her voice was soft, low and beguiling. She wore no make-up, which was unusual in those days when most girls rouged their faces when going to a dance. The main subject of conversation, as far as I recall, was about Blythe and the

Abbey. Attacking Blythe nearly ranked as a national pastime in those days, but to the surprise of a fellow like me who had had the cheek to criticise him in the magazine *Comhar,* Siobhán was like a tigress in his defence. While she admitted that he interfered in the casting and direction of plays, and corrected the players at rehearsal for mispronunciations in Irish, she said that were it not for Blythe the Abbey would be little more than a training ground for the English repertory theatres and B-grade British films. That was a career she seemed determined to avoid.

I got to know Siobhán better when I scripted the first Abbey pantomime, *Muireann agus an Prionnsa,* for Christmas 1945. Based on Lady Gregory's fantasy, *The Golden Apple,* Blythe had commissioned me to write the main script, although he himself did the translation of songs like "The Isle of Capri" and "I've Got a Gal in Kalamazoo", which were sung by a glamour girl, Pampóg, played ravishingly by Maíre Ní Dhomhnaill. Scheduled to run for six nights, the Abbey was packed for six weeks, mainly due to Frank Dermody's flawless direction. Siobhán, as Jimín, a Dublin newspaper boy, with her tresses coiled under a cap and the butt of a cigarette in the corner of her mouth, was a typical Moore Street *gamin* or jemser, who succeeded in speaking Irish with a Dublin accent without losing a titter of the humour. Liam Ó Briain, a born Dubliner who had mastered Connemara Irish, told Siobhán that she had achieved on stage something he believed impossible. The *Evening Herald* reported: "Siobhán McKenna's Jimín, son of a Moore Street trader, is a fascinating amalgam of Richmal Crompton's William and a Dublin Dead-End Kid. This is a performance of inexhaustible vitality."

The small part of a gardener in the Phoenix Park was played by Denis O'Dea, one of the outstanding Abbey actors of his generation. He took more than a fatherly interest in Siobhán's progress. He kept a wary and warning eye on would-be Clark Gables who tried to date her.

Denis O'Dea was born in the Rotunda Hospital, Dublin, on 26 April 1903, the only child of Michael O'Dea (formerly Dee), a member of the Royal Irish Constabulary, from near Causeway in north Kerry. His wife Katherine Neilan was from the nearby district of Knapogue, Ballyduff. At the time of Denis's birth they lived at Desmond Place on the north side of the city, but after he retired Michael O'Dea and family lived with his sister-in-law, Miss

Josephine Neilan, who ran a boarding house and flats in a late-Georgian house at 52 South Richmond Street, which Denis always regarded as his home. He attended the well-known Christian Brothers School in nearby Synge Street. As a young man he joined the G Company of the Third Battalion of the IRA. During the Civil War he was arrested after an ambush in St Stephen's Green when a bystander was killed. The nineteen-year-old O'Dea was interned in Newbridge Barracks, where he and his fellow prisoners staged plays like *The Coiner* and *Meadowsweet* on an improvised stage in the dining hall. After his release he and other ex-internees staged plays at the Rotunda Hall and other venues around Dublin to raise funds for the dependants of Republican prisoners. One of his close friends from those troubled years was the future Taoiseach, Seán Lemass.

He attended the Abbey School of Acting, and made his first appearance on the Abbey stage in Margaret O'Leary's *The Woman* in September 1929. As a juvenile lead he created such parts as Luke Duffy in *The New Gossoon* and Darell Blake in *The Moon in the Yellow River*. He went on Abbey tours of the United States in 1932 and 1938 and took part in John Ford's Hollywood film of *The Plough and the Stars*. A strikingly handsome figure, he was also a sportsman, punter and expert poker player. Reticent to the point of self-effacement, his generosity to less fortunate actors is still part of Abbey lore. On one occasion when they were playing together in *The New Gossoon*, Denis got a last-minute tip for a greyhound running at Harold's Cross. Siobhán was free until the third act, so she was hurriedly sent to the track by bicycle to place a good bet for Denis and to get back before she was due to appear as Sally Hamill. She duly arrived and dashed on stage breathless and a little dejected. "The minute you came on stage," Denis told her later, "I knew the dog was beaten."

Although nobody seemed aware of O'Dea's close relationship with Siobhán, they had been secretly engaged for nearly two years. Nearly forty years later she put another gloss on the secret romance. After being reprimanded by her idol, F.J. McCormick, for giggling inappropriately in a scene with him, she was still "bawling crying" when she went to collect her old bike to go home:

> Denis O'Dea followed me out and said, "You can't go home on your bicycle like that, you'll have an accident – I'll take you home in a taxi," and I said, "What a kind man."

He began to ask her to go to races with him and her father burned up the road between Galway and Dublin. "He came to Dublin a lot."[10]

They were married in Salthill, Galway, in September 1946. It was a quiet, non-theatrical event. Siobhán's sister Nancy, who had qualified as a dentist, was bridesmaid and Denis's friend, Patrick Cahill of a well-known Dublin pharmaceutical firm, was best man. The former president of University College Galway, Monsignor Hynes, was the celebrant. Siobhán's parents, not unaware of the strains which the theatre imposed on relationships, were doubly concerned that she should marry an actor, then in his prime but nearly twenty years older than she. Hardened and disillusioned actors spoke of May's marriage to September, and muttered grimly about "Autumn Fire", and "Desire Under the Elms". Siobhán did not greatly care what anybody thought or said. They were in love and marriage was a luxury they felt they could afford. Earlier that year Siobhán had had a small but rewarding part in her first film, *Hungry Hill,* while Denis had played the important part of a policeman in *Odd Man Out*, the Carol Reed masterpiece which brought F.J. McCormick belated international acclaim for his performance as "Shell".

When McCormick died of a brain tumour at the untimely age of 57, on 24 April 1947, it seemed that a gallery of unforgettable characters went with him to the grave. Siobhán in a tribute remarked that in the film world, when they offer a part in a poor script, "they try to make up for it by getting names of big stars to play opposite you. However, it doesn't work with me. They forget that I have played with one of the greatest actors in the world on the Abbey stage. My big regret is that I never made a film with F.J. – I only brushed shoulders with him in *Hungry Hill*, but wherever I go, I shall bring his memory and teachings with me."[11]

She had already made her London stage debut at the Embassy Theatre as Nora Fintry in Paul Vincent Carroll's *The White Steed*. She was perceptively noticed as an impressive newcomer by Clive Barnes who later became the greatly feared critic of the *New York Times*.

A co-starring role in a Paramount film, *Daughter of Darkness* with Beatrix Lehmann, won her instant acclaim. The screenplay, based on a stage piece of melodramatic hokum, *They Walk Alone* by Max Catto, was deservedly panned by the critics, but filmgoers

28

rushed to the box office to see what the publicity boys described as a "back of the barn Irish seductress who exerts a lethal charm for the local lads". Greatly daring, the film critic of *The Standard*, an Irish Catholic weekly, wrote of her as "a bucolic nymphomaniac – brought up in a priest's household but given to bad thoughts". Whenever this Jezebel hears organ music, she makes a grab at the nearest man. Banished by the villagers to perfidious Albion, she succumbs to the embraces of three Yorkshire yokels but solves her polygamous urges by murdering all three. Retribution is at hand when an Alsatian grabs the Irish colleen by the throat, doing the hangman out of a job. According to *Picturegoer*, the dog had already been awarded the Dickin medal, the canine VC, for rescue work in the London blitz.[12]

Paramount Films issued a special release to inform cinemagoers that the first name of the new actress should be pronounced "Shevawn, Gaelic for Josephine". The *Thames Valley Times* suggested "Chuvawn", while *Picturegoer* opted for "Sheeovan, Erse for Susan". Whatever she was called, and despite the blood-curdling improbabilities of the plot, *Daughter of Darkness* placed Siobhán on the first landing of the rickety staircase to stardom.

After their marriage, Siobhán and Denis lived for a time in a flat in Harcourt Street, Dublin, but during the filming of *Daughter of Darkness* they moved to fashionable Chelsea, on the Thames. At the time, Denis played supporting parts in two films, *The Mark of Cain* with Eric Portman and *The Last Illusion* with Ralph Richardson. Although Siobhán had several Hollywood offers, she was now pregnant and settled for a production, *Mary Rose*, which had been her choice for her audition, at the Abbey Theatre in March 1948. Denis appeared in a character part and Walter Macken, her first director at An Taibhdhearc and now a member of the Abbey company, was a Scottish clergyman. A very young and talented director, Tomás MacAnna, had been engaged for the production of plays in Irish. Forty-five years later he recalled:

> I first met Siobhán when she and her husband Denis came to see *Réalt Diarmada*, a not very successful *geamaireacht* [pantomime] at the Abbey in 1948. I knew she had done a translation of *Mary Rose* by J.M. Barrie for the Taibhdhearc some years before and I asked her whether she would come back to the Abbey (together

with her husband, Denis) and she agreed. At that time she was expecting her son Donnacha; nevertheless she came and played the part in settings by Carl Bonn (who said he didn't mind costuming Siobhán but didn't see why he should have to costume her family as well!). I became aware at the time of a certain antagonism between her and Earnán [Blythe]. I think it went back to some disagreement during the pantomime – the first one, *Muireann agus an Prionnsa*. As it happened, Earnán, as was his wont, corrected her Gaelic [in the script], causing her to walk out at the first reading in the green room. Denis and I managed to coax her back on the assurance that the script would not be tampered with. I found her easy to work with – after all, I was only a beginner in the professional theatre; she did insist on being consulted about the casting but accepted Micheál Ó hAonghusa to play opposite her (in spite of both Seamas Locke and Wally Macken's claims to the part) ... I would regard her as a most compelling personality, she filled the stage, so to speak, and was always conscious of the part; she was truly a star. I don't think she had much of an opinion of me as a director. She admired Frank Dermody immensely but was so-so about Hilton Edwards ...[13]

She must have been disappointed that the attendances were poor for the one-week run. Apart from the pregnancy, she got appendicitis but continued playing. "The skirt fell off me at the matinée on Saturday after a very dramatic scene. Luckily I kept my presence of mind."

Her only child, Donnacha (Denis), was born on 30 August 1948, and after she left the nursing home she had the services of a children's nurse. Parenthood and domesticity did not greatly interrupt her film career, on which she had set her hopes at this particular time. She was back in London in 1949 to make *The Lost People* with Denis Price and Lillian Hartnell, a film which few liked, apart from herself. Her next movie, *The Adventuress*, again with Denis Price, gave her less satisfaction. Of her performance as an English woman, *Picturegoer* used that damning word "efficient". In short, her film career plummeted after *Daughter of Darkness*. She did not help matters by refusing to sign a contract with any of the big film studios. She wanted to be free to go back to Dublin whenever no suitable part was on offer. Although she may not have realised it, she was a stage-actress moonlighting in the film studios. The technology of a director's medium seemed to circumscribe and diminish her and film producers soon lost interest in an actress who was never quite sure when she could be on the set.

Siobhán was determined that, at least on stage, she would not be typecast as the colleen with the brogue. She sought opportunities to play English parts, at least those requiring a neutral accent. Sir Laurence Olivier had invited her to play in *Fading Mansions*, Donagh MacDonagh's adaptation of Jean Anouilh's *Romeo et Jeanette*, but this was no real test as MacDonagh had transplanted the play from Brittany to Mayo. Before she finally accepted, Siobhán decided to play the lead in a limited run of the very English romantic piece *Berkeley Square* at the Cue Theatre. Olivier was not present on the first night but his associates were greatly pleased with her performance and looked forward to her success in *Fading Mansions*. When Olivier returned to London he went to see her in a matinée when Murphy's Law came into force for Siobhán – everything that could go wrong did go wrong. Her leading man, Douglas Montgomery, accidentally stood on her trailing gown, splitting the back seams. She had to try to hold it together during their big love scene. An unnerved Montgomery with a swoop of his hand brushed against her false curls and they finished on the floor. Knowing that Olivier was out front only added to Siobhán's panic and she went to pieces. He was taken aback at her lack of resource and inexperience in a situation which confronts all actors sooner or later. A production meeting was called to reconsider her suitability for the part in *Fading Mansions*, but his co-backers reassured Olivier that her earlier performances had sparkled.

Under Sir Laurence Olivier's management, *Fading Mansions* opened at the Duchess Theatre on 31 August 1949 before a distinguished audience including Vivien Leigh, Margaret Lockwood, Denis Price, Denis O'Dea, Donagh MacDonagh and Ernie O'Malley. Unlike a packed jury, a packed house of celebrities does not ensure the required verdict. Milton Shulman, the *Evening Standard* critic, complained about this transfer from a Gallic to a Gaelic setting:

The Irish are a convenient dramatic device for the Anglo-Saxon race. Whenever the characters are too wild-eyed, too eccentric, too garrulous, or too passionate to be credible as English, Scottish, Welsh or American, it is relatively safe to pour them into a Hibernian mould ...

31

When Sheila Joyce ushers her fiancé, a stiff upright Belfast business man, and her prospective mother-in-law into the decaying squalid Joyce home in Western Ireland, we soon understand why she is so apprehensive about their meeting the family.

The father is a worthless talkative old man with the appearance of an impoverished Kentucky colonel who has been hitting the mint juleps too hard. The brother is a disillusioned slovenly comic given to bitter, philosophical speeches about life, and the wife who deserted him for a "red-nosed, pot-bellied" Englishman.

The sister, Maura, is not only lazy, moody, dirty and contemptuous, but she gives herself freely to the men of the neighbourhood. By the end of the first scene one is beginning to feel that this play should have been renamed Potato Road. ... Siobhán McKenna is a wild and impassioned Maura, spitting venom from her blazing eyes, breathing poetry in each gesture, inflection and movement.[14]

An even more cynical reviewer added that Siobhán "seems to have discovered the secret of perpetual emotion".

Having more or less succeeded in re-enacting her film performance in *Daughter of Darkness* on stage at the Duchess, she received fan-mail from scores of young men and gushing letters from the other actors in the cast, including Michael Gough. An anonymous admirer summed up neatly the off-stage Siobhán of those days.

It's very hard to say what goes on under that red thatch. She wrinkles up her forehead into a worried expression, looks one straight in the eye, and then smiles a smile that knocks me sideways – the Mona Lisa was just a piker.

She was still trying to avoid the stage-Irish stereotype, so popular in the West End and on Broadway, when she opted to play the eponymous part in *Héloïse* by James Forsyth at the Duke of York's Theatre in 1951, only to get a critical thrashing from the young and acerbic critic of the *Observer*, Kenneth Tynan. Of Siobhán's Héloïse and the even more unfortunate Walter Macken's Abelard, Tynan wrote:

Their love scenes kept reminding me of the *aperçu* about Jane Welsh and Thomas Carlyle, that it is as well that they married each other since that meant two unhappy people instead of four. Mr Forsyth engineers a nocturnal tryst for them by having

Abelard awaken Héloïse by knocking something over and once they are together, the poetry begins to stand out rather like a vein on one's forehead. Their rapture smells of old, unopened rooms ... Siobhán McKenna, flinty of mein, offers a pinched Héloïse which, in its pallor and intensity, recalls the spooky lady in Charles Addams's drawings. Walter Macken invests Abelard with a soft Celtic guilt as soothing and as antiseptic as a bandage ... The direction, by Michael Powell, has a sepulchral relevance of its own, and bears traces of the film studios in that it seemed to be taking a whole working day to get through four minutes of action.[15]

Siobhán had returned to the Abbey for a guest appearance in the spring of 1950, to play the title role of Yeats's *The Countess Cathleen*. She was not billed as a guest artist and she would scarcely expect to be billed as such in the light of her constant praise of the ensemble playing at the Abbey. She frequently reminded interviewers that "the Abbey Theatre believed in serving the author faithfully and unselfishly, and hence they inevitably served themselves, developing a wonderful sense of teamwork. No actor got billing; yet to me they all had star quality, even carrying a tray."

The only concession to her success in *Daughter of Darkness* was the appearance of the name Siobhán McKenna for the first time on an Abbey programme. Previously, whether playing in Irish or English, she had been billed as Siobhán Nic Chionnaith, in accordance with the practice during the Blythe years. The director on this occasion was Ria Mooney, an excellent actress who had specialised in the production of verse plays with Austin Clarke's Lyric Theatre before she became resident director at the Abbey. From the first rehearsal Siobhán was unhappy in the part, as she failed to respond to Ria Mooney's insistence on a particular rhythm and pace for delivery of the verse.

I met Ria one morning when she told me that she was greatly worried about how to dress Siobhán for her part. The Abbey in those days had a wardrobe mistress but no regular costume designers and an overworked Ria had taken on the task:

"I went to Brown Thomas's in search of suitable material. I pondered over purple and gold and green and could not make up my mind until the counter-assistant said it was closing time. On the dot, I distinctly heard the voice of Yeats booming in my ear: 'Ria, it must be green.'"

Despite Yeats's intervention in the choice of a colour which theatre people regarded as unlucky as a quote from *Macbeth*, Siobhán was encased in a green velour gown in which she squiggled and squirmed visibly. The *Irish Press* review was tepid:

> Of such ethereal quality is Cathleen that it would taken an exceptional actress to catch that elusiveness. Siobhán McKenna's Cathleen was beautifully poised, the lines spoken with much intent but the outlines she created never quite filled one's imagination completely.[16]

K (Seamus Kelly) in *The Irish Times* succeeded in being prophetic and perceptive in his disapproval:

> Miss Siobhán McKenna's interpretation of the name part failed to move me. Miss McKenna is a fine dramatic actress, a forceful and intelligent and emotional actress, and an actress who if cast opposite Cyril Cusack might give us the greatest Pegeen Mike since Máire O'Neill. That she had worked intensively and intelligently on the part of Cathleen is evident but there is too much emotional *brio*, too many key-changes from *pianissimo* to *fortissimo* and not quite enough of the unshakeable spiritual strength mastering physical frailty which is the essential Cathleen and which is best conveyed in quiet speech and with the minimum of movement.[17]

One never associated physical frailty with Siobhán, nor the minimum of movement from a player who dominated a stage like she did. But Seamus Kelly was certainly right in his prediction about Pegeen Mike. Some in the audience would have remembered Eithne Dunne's luminous performance as the Countess in a better orchestrated production by Ria Mooney for the Lyric Theatre a few years earlier. With splendid speaking of the verse, Eithne Dunne also brought a visually exotic quality to the part which evoked Harry Clarke's stained-glass depiction of the Countess in his famous Geneva window.

Sadly, it was Siobhán's last and perhaps least successful appearance in the old Abbey Theatre. A few hours after the curtain had fallen on a production of *The Plough and the Stars* with the British Tommies singing "Keep the Home Fires Burning," the stage and auditorium were destroyed by fire in the early hours of 18 July

1951. Siobhán was playing in Scotland at the time, but a great part of her youth was buried beneath the ashes and the rubble. From her scarcely noticed debut in *Stiana* she had established herself at the Abbey as a player who really counted. She returned in triumph to the new Abbey built on the original site to play Cass in *The Loves of Cass Maguire* in 1967. In the seventeen years of absence, the professor's daughter had undergone a metamorphosis. From the beginning of her career, she had always seemed uncannily certain about what she should and should not do. Her decision to return to An Taibhdhearc in 1950 to play the lead in her own translation of one of the great plays of this century, Shaw's *Saint Joan*, was daring, quixotic and a portent in the annals of theatre.

Notes

1. James Joyce, *Pomes Penyeach* (Faber & Faber, 1966) p.16
2. *Sunday Independent*, 17 November 1986
3. Siobhán McKenna, "Belfast of My Nostalgia," *Irish Press*, 13 November 1969
4. Ibid.
5. Ibid.
6. Ibid.
7. Ibid.
8. Ibid.
9. Ibid.
10. Deirdre Purcell, interview with Siobhán McKenna, *Sunday Tribune*, December 1985, reprinted 23 November 1986
11. Gabriel Fallon, interview with Siobhán McKenna, Radió Éireann, 26 April 1947
12. *Picturegoer*, 28 February 1948
13. Tomás MacAnna, unpublished personal reminiscences, January 1993
14. *Evening Standard*, 2 September 1949
15. Kenneth Tynan, *Curtains* (Longman, 1961) pp.15-16
16. T.M. [Tony Molloy] *Irish Press*, 21 February 1950
17. *Irish Times*, 25 February 1950

Taking Wing

THE STORY OF Joan of Arc is a mystery which every age, whether in a spirit of faith or of scepticism, has tried to solve. Bernard Shaw wrote that Joan took possession of his pen as soon as he commenced his play about her, which he completed in 1923 in the Eccles Hotel, Glengarriff, Co. Cork, and in the Great Southern Hotel at Parknasilla, Co. Kerry. Even Winston Churchill, in his *History of the English Speaking Peoples*, celebrated her simple faith and valour:

> There now appeared upon the ravaged scene an Angel of Deliverance, the noblest patriot of France, the most splendid of all her heroes, the most beloved of her saints, the most inspiring of all her memories, the peasant Maid, the ever shining, ever glorious Joan of Arc. ... She glorifies as she freed the soil from which she sprang. All soldiers should read her story and ponder on the words and deeds of a true warrior, who in a single year, though untaught in technical arts, reveals in every situation the key to victory.

Joan's triumphs in battle naturally appealed to Churchill, but he by no means dismissed her supernatural authority. Neither did Bernard Shaw when he wrote in the preface to his play:

> Consider the career of Joan. She was a village girl in authority

37

over sheep and pigs, dogs and chickens, and to some extent her father's hired labourers, when he hired any, but over no one else on earth. Outside the farm, she had no authority, no prestige, no claim to the smallest deference. Yet she ordered everybody about from her uncle to the king, the archbishop and the military general staff. Her uncle obeyed her like a sheep, and took her to the castle of the local commander who in being ordered about, tried to assert himself, but soon collapsed and obeyed. And so on up to the king, as we have seen. This would have been unbearably irritating even if her orders had been offered as rational solutions of the desperate difficulties in which her social superiors found themselves just then. But they were not so offered. Nor were they offered as the expressions of Joan's arbitrary will. It was never "I say so", but always "God says so".[1]

The legendary Joan of Arc would seem irresistible as a star role for actresses, but it is surprising how few stars have attempted the part on the international stage. It may well be that by the time a stage actress has acquired the experience and technique to play the maid from Domremy, she will be nearer to thirty-nine than nineteen. Dame Sybil Thorndike, for whom Shaw wrote the part, was forty-two when she first played it in London in 1924. She was not, however, the first to play Shaw's Saint Joan; the distinction goes to Winifred Lenihan who played it in New York in the Fall of 1923. Sarah Bernhardt was forty-five and a grandmother when she played the Jules Barbier version of *Jeanne D'Arc* in Paris in 1890. Grandmother or not, when asked in the trial scene to state her age, she announced to the audience "Nineteen", bringing the house down with applause.

Siobhán McKenna was a confident and sturdy twenty-eight when she attempted the impossible in support of a seemingly lost cause – the rescue of An Taibhdhearc where she had served her apprenticeship. The little theatre was struggling to survive on an inadequate grant of £2,000 a year, staging play after play in a language of minority interest, and in competition with the cinema, dancehalls, and plays in English staged not only by professional touring companies but by a flourishing amateur dramatic movement that had begun to organise festivals on a competitive basis. Seán Ó hÓráin (Johnny Horan), who was then in charge at An Taibhdhearc, asked Siobhán, in desperation, if she could do something to save the theatre. "We're practically finished," he told her.

"I knew what he meant," Siobhán admitted. "I remembered my early days with An Taibhdhearc, the theatre my father had allowed me to join, not so that I could become an actress, but so that I could perfect my Irish. I remembered playing for two hours before an audience of one woman and her two children. I said to Johnny, 'Let's do a Joan of Arc play.'

"I read them all: Claudel's Joan at the Stake, Maxwell Anderson's Joan of Lorraine, Shaw's Saint Joan! Shaw, the deeply religious man whom many had called an atheist, had called her Saint!"[2]

Siobhán had not read Jean Anouilh's Joan of Arc play *L'Alouette*, later to win wide acclaim in Lillian Hellman's English version *The Lark*. She was intent on staging in Irish Shaw's brilliant reconstruction of the age-long dichotomy between church and state, illuminated by irony and eloquence, making it one of the most impressive achievements of twentieth-century playwriting.

The Taibhdhearc wrote to Shaw seeking permission for Siobhán's translation and the proposed production. The postcard reply read:

I don't see any sense in the Irish language revival. But if anybody goes to the trouble of translating my plays into that language, I won't bother to charge a fee.[3]

Siobhán began to translate with the help of Máire Nic Giolla Mhairtín, the actress-housekeeper. "I wrote in straight, simple language so that the Gaelic absorbed Shaw's words."[4] Siobhán believed that Shaw had the rhythms of Irish speech in his mind when he wrote the lines for a peasant Joan in Glengarriff and Parknasilla. She could not understand how he came to accept Dame Sybil Thorndike's assumed Lancashire accent, "a dialect more associated with factory or mill-girls than with peasants".[5] However, Siobhán was most likely thinking of Gracie Fields and her ill-starred attempt to film Synge's *Riders to the Sea*.

Here is a short extract from her unpublished translation of one of the most famous passages in the play, when Joan replies to her inquisitors. Shaw never presumed to write in verse, but it would be fairer to say that he wrote poetry in prose, so making easier the task of the translator. It is not a strictly literal version.

Siobhán: D'fhéadfainn déanamh gan mo chapall cogaidh; d'fhéadfainn sciorta a tharraing 'mo dhiaidh; d'fhéadfainn ligint dos na meirgí agus na ridirí agus saighdúirí dul tharram agus mé d'fhágáil 'na dhiaidh fé mar a fhágann siad na mná eile, bíodh is

39

go bhféadfainn éisteacht go fóill leis an ngaoith 'sna crainnte, na fuiseoga i solas na gréine, na huain óga ag caoineadh in aeir folláin seaca, agus cloigeanna beannaithe an tséipéil a chuireann mo ghuthaí ainglithe ag bog-ghluaiseacht chugam ar an ngaoith. Ach in éagmais na rudaí seo, ní thig liom maireachtaint, agus de bhrí go bhfuil sibh ag iarraidh iad a thógáil uaim-se nó ó neach ar bith, is fios dom go bhfuil bhúr gcomhairle ón diabhal agus mo chuid-se ó Dhia.

Joan: I could do without my warhorse. I could drag about in a skirt; I could let the banners and the knights and the drummers pass me and leave me behind as they leave the other women, if only I could still hear the wind in the trees, the larks in the sunshine, the young lambs crying through the healthy frost, and the blessed, blessed church bells that send my angel voices floating to me on the wind. But without these things I cannot live; and by your wanting to take them away from me, or from any hungry creature, I know that your counsel is of the devil and that mine is of God.

Siobhán's enthusiastic return brought new life to An Taibhdhearc. Not since 1928, when Micheál MacLiammóir and Hilton Edwards, with a motley crew, staged *Diarmuid agus Gráinne* had such a galli-maufry of diverse talents assembled in Middle Street. Ian Priestley Mitchell, an English actor of the Sir John Martin Harvey school and a cooing compère of the Irish Hospital Sweepstakes radio programme, was engaged as director despite his protestations that he had not a word of Irish. He had managed ENSA tours for the troops in Northern Ireland during the war and was expected to keep order at rehearsals, especially amongst the extras from the Irish-speaking battalion from Renmore Barracks and the less disciplined college students. When matters sometimes got out of hand he stopped the play by blowing furiously on a referee's whistle, as the boys in the crowd scenes refused to accept direction in English. Poor Ian's predicament was a source of amusement to the locals, especially when he told the lot of them that he was "no bleddy Sasanach" but of one of the Border clans who had rallied to the cause of Bonnie Prince Charlie. It was no great surprise that when Ian went down with flu Siobhán took over as director, assisted by a Welshman, the stage designer Chris Landon Sorrell, who gave his services free. The programme generously credited Ian Priestley

Mitchell as *Léiritheoir* (Director) although he had only planned the moves. Seán Ó hÓráin, Liam Ó Briain, Breandán Ó Tighearnaigh and the other principal players rallied to Siobhán's support. As she gained confidence, she dropped the professor of English, Diarmuid Ó Murchú, from the cast because he did not know his lines at the dress rehearsal. Using an old Abbey production formula that in key scenes nobody should move except the character who was speaking, Siobhán brought order out of chaos. Tommy King, the stage carpenter, and her friend Aggie Moran looked after the props and the making of the costumes.

That Christmas production in 1950 was a notable occasion at An Taibhdhearc. The President of Ireland, Seán T. Ó Ceallaigh, attended and was seated on a raised dais in the front stalls so that the little man could have an uninterrupted view of the stage. Later, Siobhán used to say facetiously that she never took her eyes off of him in case he would fall off his perch. Ernest Blythe suggested that Siobhán should play the part with the Abbey company, but she remained loyal to her Taibhdhearc cast who had played to packed houses. She even succeeded in persuading Louis Elliman of the Gaiety Theatre to give her a Sunday night booking for the Taibhdhearc production in early January 1951.

It was not the first time that plays in Irish had been staged at the Gaiety. As long ago as October 1901 the Irish Literary Theatre, a forerunner of the Abbey, had staged Douglas Hyde's *Casadh an tSúgáin* at that venue. Siobhán's bold stroke meant that Dublin *Gaeilgeoirí* and many Connemara people living in Dublin felt compelled to go to the Gaiety just as they flocked to Croke Park when Galway was playing.

The transfer of the Taibhdhearc production to the Gaiety was jeopardised by a rail strike and a winter blizzard which made road transport perilous. Again Renmore Barracks came to the rescue, when two days before the performance the Minister for Defence gave permission for the use of army lorries to transport scenery, props and costumes. Siobhán recalled:

I shall never forget the confusion; somehow we gathered the lorries and gathered the cars with chains for the icy roads. Six lorries stood ready. And behind them were dozens of Galway cars as citizens caught the fever of the drama.

We set off through the snow and the wind and over the ice. Car after car, lorry after lorry broke down. Everyone tumbled out to push. We jacked up. We changed tyres. We battled through Athlone and Mullingar.

At Lucan, we began changing for our first dress rehearsal ... changing in the lorries. Up Grafton Street moved an army of Irish, French and English soldiers, fresh from the middle centuries. The Gaiety waived its rule so that more could stand in the aisles. Jimmy O'Dea gave me his dressing room ... We played *San Siobhán* and the critics raved. So much so that Sir Laurence Olivier wrote to me that the St James's Theatre was "available". London was beckoning an Irish Saint Joan.

What a blow for Ireland! But the blow came the other way. The army men were recalled and the project died as gallant and weary soldiers drove back to barracks.

But Joan had not finished with me![6]

Most of the reviews were in Irish as the newspapers had regular contributors for Irish plays in those years. Not surprisingly, they lavished praise on the venture, and parts of Siobhán's translation were published with illustrations in the *Sunday Press*. R.M. Fox, an English socialist and critic, summed up in the *Evening Mail*:

To say that Siobhán McKenna dwarfed the others in the cast is not to take away from their stature for they gave her excellent support. But it does mean that we have an actress capable of maintaining heavy emotional roles. That she has done this in an Irish play of her own translation adds piquancy to her triumph. She has given an effective answer to those who complained of the dullness of recent Irish drama.[7]

An Taibhdhearc had once more come to the notice of the public. But *San Siobhán* was a one-off *tour de force* which could not be repeated. Siobhán had shown her incredible energy. She could rehearse all day, or travel like a fit-up actor, and go on the stage that night with a poise and a radiance that enthralled. She was not just an actress playing a part in an obscure language, she was a Saint Joan who seemed capable of making every utterance and intonation intelligible even to those whose knowledge of the spoken tongue was slight. Nothing could be more rebellious and at the same time so poetic as her impassioned defence of her "voices" in defiance of the English. Siobhán frequently said that she modelled Joan on her mother, a woman of unquestionable faith who could virtually browbeat God into answering her intentions:

> She would be talking and would suddenly turn away from us and say: "Now, look here, I have never refused anything You asked me. I am just insisting that You do this one thing for me." She would talk to God quite frankly, and extraordinary things would happen. My father went from Belfast to Galway as a university lecturer in mathematics and when the Chair of Mathematical Physics became vacant, my mother told him: "You must go for that, Eoin!" "Don't be silly, woman," he answered, but he went. My mother told him he would get thirteen votes. "Don't be talking through your hat," he said, "I'll get about eight." But she insisted, "You'll get about thirteen because I've heard thirteen masses this morning." That evening about six o'clock we were sitting down to tea when there was a knock at the door. My father, all nerves, went to open it and we heard a voice saying: "Congratulations." My mother rose like a queen from the table and called out to ask: "How many votes?" My sister Nancy and I were stunned to hear: "Thirteen." It was all totally real to my mother. Shaw's definition of a miracle is something strange to those who witness it and simple to those who perform it. I am sure it has something to do with prayer, and prayer could be just wishing. My mother had this extraordinary faith and complete acceptance, which used to get on my father's nerves sometimes. I remember him turning to her one day when she said: "Welcome to the will of God," and remarking: "Greta, do you know what it is? If this house fell down on top of us you would say 'Welcome to the will of God.' And my mother insisted, "I would because there would be nothing else you could say!" She was like Joan. You couldn't answer back because she had this remarkable common sense.[8]

That gentle woman, whom Siobhán regarded as a sensible saint, broke a hip and was bed-ridden for many months before her death in 1952. It came as something of a surprise to Siobhán and her sister Nancy when her father married his young secretarial assistant, Cathleen O'Connor, soon afterwards. He had been a true father-figure for Siobhán, to an overpowering extent in her formative years. She inherited from him a sharp mind and a respect for scholarship, but it was her devout and devoted mother who respected Siobhán's choice of acting as a vocation. After their mother's death, the old house in Fort Eyre was never quite the same for Nancy and Siobhán.

Brought up in a strongly nationalist tradition, Siobhán liked to contrast the problems of Ireland in the fifties with the fragmented France of Joan of Arc's time. She once claimed:

> There are a thousand girls like Joan in Ireland ... And all of them feel like Joan that the English are very nice, only they ought to stay in their own country.[9]

This may seem naive to the politically correct nowadays, but Siobhán rightly regarded theatre as primarily an emotional experience. Her Joan was Ireland's Joan. Armed with a powerful and melodious voice, she dared gestures that would look silly if not motivated by her inmost being or, as she would like to think, her "voices". For the fortunate few who saw *San Siobhán*, a great talent shone "like a tall candle in a holy place".

The Taibhdhearc success in Galway and at the Gaiety was a further drain on the finances of the O'Dea household. All might have ended in an embarrassing anti-climax were it not for the courage of Shelah Richards who had played *Saint Joan* with her own company at the Olympia Theatre during the Second World War. This former Abbey and Gate Theatre actress, on first seeing Siobhán play at the Abbey, said wryly to her companion at an interval, "At last they've got a juvenile as good as I was." Shelah had been the original Nora Clitheroe in *The Plough and the Stars* and had played Juliet to Cyril Cusack's Romeo. She was a truly unselfish admirer of Siobhán's talent and had directed her in *The White Steed* at the Embassy Theatre a few years earlier. When she joined with Lennox Robinson to form a small company to stage *The Playboy of the Western World* at the Edinburgh Theatre Festival in 1951, she knew instinctively that she had the ideal Pegeen Mike in Siobhán McKenna. The original invitation to the festival had been sent to the Abbey, but Ernest Blythe, probably on the grounds that it was a "fringe" production and not part of the main drama programme, declined to send the Abbey company to perform. Lennox Robinson felt that it was an opportunity to co-operate with Shelah Richards in assembling an ad hoc company billed as the Dublin Players to present a series of Abbey plays, including his best-known comedy, *The Whiteheaded Boy*, which he planned to direct himself.

Siobhán had only appeared once before in Synge at the Abbey when she had played the minor part of Sarah Tansey, one of the girls who came by "the stones of the river" to admire the Playboy. Shelah Richards remarked:

> I was fascinated by the idea of doing a new production of *The Playboy*. I had became very bored with the way, over the years, that the Abbey had done the play. The tradition of the early days of Máire O'Neill, Arthur Sinclair, Sara Allgood and Fred O'Donovan had been carried on into the later companies; and I felt that in recent years the play had lost its original fire and had turned rather drearily into a sing-song recitation. ... During rehearsal I found that a lot of the actors, most of whom had never seen *The Playboy*, were starting in on the old Synge-song thing. Siobhán, for instance, was utterly amazed when I said to her that what she was doing was splendid but it wasn't what I wanted. She was very young at the time, but somewhat doubtfully started doing it my way, making me stop her whenever she started the singing thing. I did, and she magnificently did what I asked her to do, and ended up giving a consummate performance in Edinburgh.[10]

The Dublin Players appeared at the Lauriston Hall, run by the Jesuit Fathers in proximity to their church and hostel. At best, it could only have been a sideshow to the Lyceum Theatre's *A Winter's Tale* with John Gielgud, had it not been for Siobhán's fiery and passionate Pegeen. Liam Gannon, an intelligent actor, played a competent Christy Mahon, while Denis O'Dea as Shawneen Keogh and Carroll O'Connor as Michael James made the most of their comedy parts.

Carroll O'Connor, then a student at Trinity College, later made a name for himself in Hollywood and on TV in the United States. He regarded Michael James as the great comedy part of all time but Shelah Richards continuously slapped him down at rehearsals for overplaying it! He made amends by leaving us his first-hand impressions of Siobhán's Pegeen Mike:

> I doubt if she ever made a more brilliant appearance on the stage. She used her magnificent voice, capable of the most wonderful contrasts – of great emotional power, and soft, deep, gentleness – as I have never heard her use it; nor have I ever seen her act more

gracefully and meaningfully. I do not mean that Siobhán will never be better. On the contrary, she is one of those rare actresses whose career will be a series of steadily improving successes to the very end. In *Playboy*, however, she found a role so beautifully written, of such completeness, that it consumed all of her immense talent, letting nothing go to waste.

Although the tour showed a small profit, the number of playgoers who saw Siobhán's first Pegeen did not greatly exceed the attendances at *San Siobhán*. Great ventures, it seems, have small beginnings. And the Edinburgh playgoers were less mannerly, according to the *Scotsman*:

> It must have been as disconcerting for this excellent company to have to compete with banging doors and coughing as it was for many in the audience to bear with acoustics which smothered some of the best lines.

The Edinburgh trip was a family outing as Siobhán and Denis brought along their three-year-old son Donnacha with his nurse Síle Ní Chonchubhair. Again Siobhán's triumph was bought at the expense of her and Denis's earnings from earlier films. Becoming increasingly publicity conscious, Siobhán remarked to a reporter from the *Daily Mail* that she was now translating *The Playboy* into Irish, with a view to repeating the success of *San Siobhán* at An Taibhdhearc. This brought an unexpected and devastating attack on her audacity from the Thersites of Irish letters, Myles na Gopaleen alias Flann O'Brien alias Brian Ó Nualláin:

> I understand she [Siobhán] now projects what is surely an unheard of literary atrocity – the translation into Irish of *The Playboy of the Western World*, presumably with herself as Pegeen Mike and Cyril Cusack as the Playboy.
> Alas, this will never do!
> ... Synge invented an English language based on Irish which rings to the foreign ear with strangeness and charm. It is strictly an export job, for any sensible person here sees through it immediately. It is just the old unfunny trick of deadpan, absolutely literal translation from one language to another – the stock English-speaking stage Frenchman, up to his oxters in words and syntax he only half understands. Play Synge's work outside the country by all means; people who laugh at the *Playboy* here are largely

laughing at themselves (not always a good thing!) and those who originally denounced the play had sounder taste than those who denounced them. The people of the West are not generally quaint clowns who cannot speak properly. Miss McKenna can prove this by proceeding with her threat to translate the *Playboy* into Irish! Then we shall see!¹¹

No more was heard of Siobhán's "threat", although others had attempted translations which only added substance to Myles na Gopaleen's tirade. Like Seamus Kelly earlier, Myles showed one prophetic touch in linking Cyril Cusack and Siobhán as Christy Mahon and Pegeen Mike, an inspired theatrical pairing still waiting in the wings.

Always ambitious to extend her range outside peasant parts and the sexy hoydens she was asked to portray in films, Siobhán accepted an invitation to play a nine-month Shakespearean season at Stratford-upon-Avon in 1952. The first Irish actress invited to play a full season there, she played supporting roles in *As You Like It*, *Coriolanus* and *Macbeth* in a company which included Sir Ralph Richardson, Margaret Leighton, Anthony Quayle and Laurence Harvey under the direction of Glen Byam Shaw. This was the first occasion when she expressed dissatisfaction with her manager, Bernard McGinn, an old Dublin friend who worked for a time with the acting agency Linnit and Dunfee. Friendship, she realised, was no real basis for what should have been a formal business relationship in a highly competitive profession and she signed up with Al Parker, who had had Denis O'Dea on his books for some years. The season at Stratford-upon-Avon involved a long absence from Dublin, so Denis went to live with his aunt at his old home in South Richmond Street. Siobhán never liked the house which was situated on a busy street and did not think it a healthy place for young Donnacha to grow up. All through those years she was determined to make Dublin her permanent home. She decided that a career on stage would be more lasting than the film appearances which she knew by now to be "obviously very transitory".

Equally transitory was her first provincial tour in England as the blonde Avril in Sean O'Casey's *Purple Dust*, directed by Sam Wanamaker. The try-out dates in Glasgow, Edinburgh, Blackpool and Brighton were intended as a run-in for a London première at the Mermaid Theatre under the management of Bernard Miles. O'Casey attended some of the preliminary rehearsals in London in April 1953 where he met Siobhán for the first time. Her old ex-Abbey colleagues Eithne Dunne, Liam Redmond and Seamus Locke were also in the cast. Siobhán's comments on their off-stage parleys with O'Casey are incisive and amusing. She saw through the Socratic irony of O'Casey's defence of Maria Duce, a right-wing Dublin Catholic organisation and a self-appointed moral censor of literature and the stage. O'Casey also professed his admiration for "Archbishop McQuaid's splendid Lenten Pastoral".

Writing to her husband from London, Siobhán revealed:

> He [O'Casey] says the Maria Duces are the only true Catholics in Ireland, carrying out Canon Law. I said "What Canon Law?" He admired Archbishop McQuaid immensely. If I printed two of the things he [O'Casey] said, he'd be a liquidated communist in earnest. He said you must make a fine Canon in *Shadow and Substance*. Later he admitted that he had never seen you. Liam [Redmond] sums up his contradictory character admirably: "Siobhán, he is a dramatist; and all dramatists have to be able to present even things they don't believe, credible to an audience whether that audience be in public or in private".[12]

When O'Casey said that F.J. McCormick was "no actor at all because he was too conscientious", Siobhán was infuriated:

> He is really a very self-conscious man, and contradicts himself all the time by saying things just for effect.[13]

O'Casey travelled to Edinburgh to see *Purple Dust* at the King's Theatre where he was disappointed at the play's unfavourable reviews while surprisingly admitting to being

> fairly full of Scotch whiskey, in addition to a special brand, called Drambudie (*sic*) – pronounced Dram-boo-ee; and full, too, of the Gaelic songs – lovely and melodious – sung informally at gatherings in this home of that Scot and that home of this Scot.[14]

Siobhán's relations with the garrulous O'Casey were not helped by her comment on the difficult touring conditions of the *Purple Dust* cast. There was a sharp retort from the playwright:

> Your mention of the Irish players making sacrifices for me disturbs me a lot as I shouldn't wish at all that any should make a sacrifice for me.[15]

Siobhán was now in no doubt that the tour was in trouble and that a London date was unlikely:

> There has been a deal of trouble between Sam [Wanamaker] and the English actors. For once, the Irish are quiet. We are still rehearsing, chopping, changing. We go to Brighton next week – Miles would prefer not to go into the West End with it as he didn't get the reviews he would have liked so far! O'Casey has rewritten some of the play to its detriment. The burning house is cut but also any other strong line in the play. Well, I exaggerate.[16]

Purple Dust never reached London. When it closed Siobhán regretted that she had gone to the trouble of dyeing her hair blonde for the part of Avril. Her natural hair had not regained its russet elegance when she began rehearsals with Cyril Cusack's new company for her first Dublin appearance as Pegeen Mike in *The Playboy* at the Gaiety Theatre, Dublin, on 20 July 1953.

In his new role as actor-manager Cusack held the trump card in having an enviable reputation as Christy Mahon which he had played opposite two earlier Abbey Pegeen Mikes, Ann Clery in the thirties and Bríd Ní Loingsigh in the early forties. Now at the zenith of his career, he was widely regarded as the most accomplished of the Abbey actors since F.J. McCormick. He had been on stage since his childhood with his "stepfather" Breffni O'Rorke and his mother Moira Breffni, a Cockney music-hall artiste. For this first *Playboy* staged under his own management, Cyril chose as director the young and relatively inexperienced actor Jack McGowran, who later became famous for his interpretations of Samuel Beckett parts. He had acquired some experience of production at the Peacock with the Abbey Experimental Theatre but he was obviously more at home in the small part of Philly Cullen, which he played with his accustomed drollery. Of McGowran's directorial skill, Cyril Cusack commented: "He had a delicate touch; he gave the kind of direction that sensitive actors would respond to." In turn, there is little doubt that McGowran responded to Cusack's finely honed individualistic approach to his own part in *The Playboy*. Carroll O'Connor, who played Jimmy Farrell in that production, credited McGowran with the introduction of musicians on stage with fiddles, melodeon and flute after the racecourse scene; but the most innovative presentation touches were the settings and costumes designed by Michael O'Herlihy.

Siobhán had now to face the first great challenge of her career in playing a barefooted Pegeen of about twenty opposite the most experienced Christy Mahon of the century, supported by a cast of all-round excellence. In the light of her Edinburgh experience, Siobhán knew instinctively that she must hold the stage from the first to the last lines of this poetic and satiric classic. She must be the muse who sets the Playboy's imagination on fire; he is after all the creation of Pegeen Mike whose love-talk inspires him to be a "hero in the end all". From his first entrance – "small, black and dirty – afeard of the polis and the walking dead" – Pegeen's infatuation with his "gallous" story of how he split his father's skull with a loy kindles the spark of poetry in him until he is ready "to go romancing through a tomping lifetime until the dawning of the judgement day". Siobhán strode the stage with a panther-like grace in pursuit of her playboy, only to see him escape her pounce at the close of the play. Pegeen knows that she has only herself to blame when the Christy Mahon of her own creation departs: "Oh, my grief, I've lost him surely, I've lost the only playboy of the western world."

Siobhán uttered this lament in a voice lowered to a whisper of infinite longing, the perfect coda to a performance of sinuous sensuality. Without Cusack's seemingly artless teamwork, she could not have reached such heights. Her immortal longings could not be stirred except by a Christy who could woo this serpent of old Nephin. Cusack's incomparable gift for underplaying allowed Siobhán, at least for once, to "capsize the stars". So began a rather fragile partnership which did not reach full fruition until they both returned to the Abbey in the late nineteen sixties and seventies.

Later there was a continental tour which included a memorable visit to the Sarah Bernhardt Theatre in Paris for an international festival when Cyril Cusack, the actor-manager, neatly upstaged Siobhán by making his curtain speech in Irish and French – something she would have clearly loved to do herself. The Irish company shared the honours of the international season with the Berliner Ensemble production of Brecht's *Mother Courage*. Pierre Aubray in the *Bulletin de Paris* discovered in the production "*le secret de l'Irlande moderne; toujours hors de monde, où au bord de monde, indomptée, inutile et illustre*". Other critics were bewildered by the wild poetic surge of Synge's language, but were clearly impressed by a distinctive acting style which they traced back to a native source, Antoine's Théâtre Libre.

Siobhán's only other appearance under Cyril Cusack's management was as Louka in Shaw's *Arms and the Man*. Her secret ambition was to play *Saint Joan* in English, but for the moment she had to be satisfied with two radio performances, in both Irish and English, with the Radio Éireann Players, both produced in 1954 by another Taibhdhearc alumnus, Seamus Breathnach. Later that year she joined the Edwards-MacLiammóir company for their season at the Gaiety Theatre, playing in Peter Ustinov's *Love of Four Colonels* and Eugene O'Neill's *Anna Christie*, and bringing new audiences to the Gaiety at a time when the Edwards-MacLiammóir company was in the doldrums. Hilton Edwards told Siobhán: "I don't bring them in, dear. Just the old ladies rattling their teacups." In the end they decided that they would do *Saint Joan*, even on a tight budget with simple but imaginative settings by Michael O'Herlihy.

On 18 November 1954 the Gaiety was packed to see how *San Siobhán* would translate to the language in which it was first written, while retaining the Connemara cadenza as a leitmotif of Siobhán's interpretation. Edwards, a master technician and tactician, gave her a free rein. MacLiammóir was an impressive Warwick with Hilton Edwards as the Bishop of Beauvais and Denis Brennan as the Bastard of Orleans heading what Dublin critics liked to describe as a strong supporting cast. Jack McGowran's Dauphin was something unique. According to Siobhán, he was exactly as Shaw described the character: "He has narrow little eyes, near together, a long pendulous nose that droops over his thick, short upper lip, and the expression of a young dog accustomed to being kicked, yet incomparable and irrepressible." Two years later Siobhán was shocked to find that McGowran had been replaced as the Dauphin by MacLiammóir for a European tour which included the Paris Theatre Festival. She tried to flatter MacLiammóir by telling him that he was too beautiful for the part, reminding him that he was never "a Bisto kid". "What she meant," explained MacLiammóir, "was that I was too old. She couldn't mother me, like she could Jackie."[17] He was, in fact, too old for the part and tried "to camp it up" by upstaging Siobhán with outrageous bits of business.

Of Siobhán's performance, the Dublin reviewers used the kind of phrases which are usually culled for media publicity: "a miracle of characterisation" ... "a wonderful *Saint Joan*, so wonderful that it is difficult to imagine a better" ... "she didn't seem to act; she seemed to be, and such was the force of her sincerity that most of the other players looked effete beside her."

Nothing fails like such success in Dublin. There were purists who disapproved of the Connemara *blas* and dear old ladies from Rathgar who spoke lovingly of their favourite Saint Joan, Dorothy Holmes-Gore, who appeared at the Gaiety with the Charles MacDona Company in 1925. Siobhán was mildly amused:

> You know, when I first went to the Abbey Theatre, everyone said I was real P.Q. I didn't know what they were talking about. At first I thought it was something vulgar, then I thought it was maybe something nice. They teased me for a long time until I finally found out it meant "Peasant Quality". I felt really complimented.[18]

She felt no need to explain her Irish slant on the part when the play went on tour to Limerick and Cork; but on their visit to Belfast she clashed with Hilton Edwards when the Opera House management wanted to play "God Save the Queen" after the show.

> "In England," Siobhán told Hilton, "I would stand. But not in Ireland. I mean no disrespect to the British Queen."
> "It would be bad manners," Hilton said.
> "If I am asked to do it," I told him, "I'll walk off."
> Hilton said I would be the cause of having all the players out of work. So I agreed ... mainly because I realised there was another way to make my protest.
> They played the British anthem that night. We all stood ... with heads bowed and eyes downcast.
> The last night of the play, I was called on to speak. I did – in Irish! You could have heard a pin drop.
> Then I switched to English. "I have been speaking in my national language. I am a Belfast native speaker ..."
> I wasn't allowed to say any more. The huge crowd, Orangemen, nationalists, loyalists, extremists, stood and cheered and cheered.
> We had won Belfast![19]

Later in 1956 she also won Paris: no mean achievement, according to the *Figaro* critic, in a city which had seen Sarah Bernhardt, Falconetti and Ludmilla Pitoeff in the part.

Shaw had told Madame Pitoeff that she had given "a wonderful representation of a scullery maid being sentenced to a fortnight's imprisonment for stealing a pint of milk for her illegitimate child". [20]

Siobhán would have dearly loved to know what Shaw himself would have said about her Connemara "voices"! She liked to believe that he had actually heard of her although he had died in 1951 on All Souls' Day when she was translating the epilogue for An Taibhdhearc. Her nearest contact with Shaw was through a Dublin Corporation dustman, Patrick O'Reilly, who lived near her at 17A Richmond Place. A lifelong correspondent with the playwright, he was the first to suggest the restoration of Shaw's birthplace in Synge Street as a museum, as a tribute from the Irish people. In thanking him, Shaw replied that the only gift he wanted from the Irish people was "their prayers, which were unpurchasable". Patrick O'Reilly told Siobhán:

> If my old friend, Bernard Shaw, was alive and seeing you acting Saint Joan – he would ask for nothing better. There's a lot of people in this town and if they were standing on their tippy toes on the highest mountain, they would not be fit to wipe GBS's boots. I would like to have a picture of you on the steps of GBS's birthplace.[21]

When the London director, John Fernald, invited Siobhán to appear at the Arts Theatre in the autumn of 1954, Siobhán was disappointed that the Gaiety cast could not appear there. Neither the theatre budget nor British Actors Equity would allow such a transfer. Moreover, John Fernald was intent on mounting his own production, with a new cast. All he wanted was Siobhán and he wanted her for a playing salary of twelve pounds a week. Her father told her that his secretary earned that. "Yes," said Siobhán, "but your secretary can't play Saint Joan!"

Again the London management raised the tiresome matter of the Irish brogue, as they called it. London, she was told, did not like the word "peasant", but once again a determined Siobhán got her own way by threatening to play the part in a broken French accent. Sir John Barbirolli told her to play it like a musician. She knew what he meant, as she explained later:

> There is fine music in *Saint Joan*. There is orchestration of voices. The trial scene actually roars. I picture the bullying Duc de Tremouille as a saxophone. I can see the Dauphin as a pathetic flute. There are fiddles and bugles and drums. There's an organ in the cathedral scene. Shaw knew his music – he was a music critic

at one time – and his knowledge of the art makes itself felt in *Saint Joan*.[22]

This was an early indication that Siobhán now considered herself as a "conductor/director" in embryo who would later try to exert directorial control in the plays in which she chose to appear.

Neither Siobhán nor John Fernald took account of those periods of unpopularity or even neglect which follow on the death of the recently famous. When *Saint Joan* opened in London there were many critics, old and new, who felt that the sage of Ayot Saint Lawrence had outlived his time and his relevance. Harold Hobson in the *Sunday Times* clearly disliked the play:

> The unpalatable truth is that a man without religion cannot write a truly religious play anymore than a man with a brain like an argumentive card index can understand emotion.[23]

Such a comment makes all the more remarkable his unqualified approval of Siobhán's performance, which he clearly preferred to impressive interpretations by Charles Lloyd Pack as the Inquisitor, Oliver Burt as the Bishop of Beauvais, Douglas Wilmer as the Earl of Warwick and Kenneth Williams as the Dauphin:

> Miss Siobhán McKenna gives to Joan the radiance, the devotion, the rapture of unseen things that her author missed; her performance is pathetic in its youth and simplicity, and when holiness descends on her, it is an authentic holiness.[24]

Kenneth Tynan of the *Observer*, then the *enfant terrible* of drama critics and the darling of the avant-garde, dismissed Shaw's play as "swagger and fustian":

> This is the first of his plays into which Shaw's senility creeps. The jokes misfire; the debates languish; and Shaw's passion for penal reform obtrudes to the detriment at the end ... She [Joan] suffers as a dramatic creation from the weakness of having no weaknesses, a divinely illuminated simpleton, she is incapable of change or development. Or so it seems on the stage. And this is where Siobhán McKenna comes in ... This actress lets us see life stripping Joan down to her spiritual buff. The beaming clown of the opening scenes has undergone by the end an annealing; all that was mortal about her has been peeled away and sheer soul bursts through. "God is alone" had tears flowing everywhere in

the house and during the epilogue one scarcely dared look at the stage. Miss McKenna's voice, with its brave Connemara twang, must somehow acquire a middle register between pp and ff; but this is my only quibble with the richest portrait of saintliness since Falconetti shaved her head for Dreyer's film *La Passion de Jeanne d'Arc*.[25]

Siobhán won lavish praise not only from what were called "the posh Sundays" but from the reviewers of the widely read popular dailies. Less concerned with Shavian metaphysics, they fixed their gaze on a new star:

If Irish actress, Siobhán McKenna, can follow up her achievement in Bernard Shaw's *Saint Joan* last night, she may become one of the greatest actresses alive.

If she never acts as well again, I shall never forget her.

She twinkles on at first as the comic, barefoot country girl who is breezily sure she can drive the English troops from France.

She looks like a scrubbed schoolboy, though her voice is soft with the cadence of her native Connemara. But the marvel is to see how she grows as Joan grows.

Among dainty courtiers, the school kid turns as sturdy and as rugged as a tree. And when the church tries her for heresy, she becomes a soul tormented. Not by doubt. But she knows now what it is to be an officer of God.

And, at the last her countenance shines with the radiance of a saint.[26]

The broadcaster and BBC critic Stephen Williams wrote of her just this side of idolatry:

I have seen many Joans, but none has entered my heart so irresistibly and irreplaceably as Siobhán McKenna did last night.

Never had I been so keenly conscious of the heartbreaking fight of the individual against the institution, or so blessedly confident that the individual will always win – although it may take centuries.

The fire that consumed Joan's body will light up her name forever. The performance has more than beauty: it has a sacred rapture.[27]

Such plaudits might have been overwhelming except that Siobhán always insisted that she never read her notices until a play had settled into a run. She did know that Sir Winston Churchill, an admirer of *Saint Joan*, came to see the show, but fortunately there was no occasion for a curtain speech. In fact, she seems to have felt a shade sorry for that great man in the front row "looking like some large elderly baby", who might think that the "dreadful words" she had to say about the English were directed at him. She always tried to remember that, despite what the critics wrote, she could not put into the play what was not there already and that neither the poetry nor the sanctity were of her making:

> Saint Joan is many people mixed into one. There is the military genius. And there is no question that she was a saint, directly inspired by God.
>
> Joan was human. She possessed warmth and to a great degree humour. What appeals to me most was her wonderful honesty and truthfulness. She was never one to flatter anybody unduly. I don't think she wanted to be a martyr. And she was too humble to realise that she was a great saint. Like you and me, she possessed fear. She did not want to be burnt. That makes her all the greater. Shaw properly put comedy into the trial scene. Otherwise, it would be too harrowing. This makes for a more rounded play.[28]

The only dissenting voice was that of the prissy and petulant Kenneth Williams, the Dauphin in the production who wrote of Siobhán's interpretation as "self-pitying and complacent – with no understanding of the Shavian dialectic".[29]

The first *Evening Standard* awards for the best London productions of 1954 excited considerable interest. The adjudicating panel consisted of Sir Michael Balcon, Milton Shulman, Harold Hobson, Rosamund Lehmann and John Fernald. This jury did not distinguish themselves by voting for *Tiger at the Gates* by Jean Giradoux in preference to Beckett's *Waiting for Godot* as the best new play. They were on more solid ground when they plumped for Richard Burton as Henry the Fifth for the best actor award. Siobhán's *Saint Joan* had transferred from the Arts Theatre to the Saint Martin's Theatre with a number of changes in the cast and had been lavished with praise at both venues. Dorothy Tutin in *The Wild Duck* and Irene Worth in *The Queen and the Rebels* were nominated by some of the jurors, but after some discussion Siobhán was the unanimous choice as best actress for "her tender and passionate Saint Joan".

The five month run of *Saint Joan* in London did not increase greatly the income of the O'Dea household. However, by Dublin standards, they lived comfortably at 52 South Richmond Street after their short stay in Chelsea. There was the occasional extravagance like the purchase of a two-year-old racehorse, trained by Morny Wing, a former champion jockey, named "Don Don" after young Donnacha. I once went to Naas races to back it, on the strength of a tip from Siobhán, but it did not finish in the first three. Denis was a well-known figure at the racetracks, and while he was an astute and successful poker player, he was less successful on the racecourse. His biggest single win on the horses was most likely the £117 he collected from the Irish Hospital Sweepstakes on an unplaced horse in the Grand National in 1949.

The O'Dea family was Irish speaking, helped by maids from the Gaeltacht, and Denis was a frequent visitor to Kruger's guesthouse in Dunquin, Co. Kerry, where he first went to improve his Irish. Siobhán's absences while working in London meant that Denis worked less frequently as an actor. He had the added responsibility of looking after Donnacha's schooling, first at Scoil Lorcán, Stillorgan, an all-Irish preparatory school, and later at the Christian Brothers, Synge Street.

Sir Alexander Korda had Siobhán in mind to star in a film of *Saint Joan*, but Shaw had given the film rights to Gabriel Pascal, the director who made *Pygmalion* an outstanding success. Pascal embarked on a search for a young and preferably unknown Saint Joan. His agent in Ireland was Frank Dermody, Siobhán's old friend from her early Abbey days. Dermody booked into the best hotels throughout the country and auditioned hundreds of teenagers whose doting mothers and bossy elocution teachers wilted under the whiplash of Dermody's "Enough, thanks! Next!"

One aspirant was encouraged when Dermody told her, "Come on! Come on! Give it to us! You can do better than that, missy."

Her elocution teacher interjected: "I was afraid that she would over-act, Mr Dermody."

"Madam," he replied, "I would remind you that you must be able to act before you can over-act."

With an age bar of twenty decreed by Pascal, Siobhán, as Denis O'Dea said, "was not at the races". Pascal died before the auditions were finished and the search for an unknown Joan switched to

America, where eventually Otto Preminger made an uninspired choice in an attractive baby doll, seventeen-year-old Jean Seberg from Iowa, for the great part.

Siobhán got film offers for one-off parts in occasional films but she refused to sign a contract with any of the major studios. She turned down offers to play the lead in several new plays including *Kathleen* by Michael Sayers, which flopped at the box-office. She had clearly set her sights on playing *Saint Joan* on Broadway, but Julie Harris was billed to appear as Joan in the Jean Anouilh version, *The Lark*, at the Longeacre Theatre in November 1955. Two Saint Joans were more than New York could stand, so Siobhán had to settle for making her American debut in Enid Bagnold's *The Chalk Garden*, which proved a fortunate choice.

She sailed on the *Mauritania* from Cork, arriving in New York on 21 August 1955, where she was met by the play's producer Irene Mayer Selznick, a leading impresario, and the film star Cary Grant, one of the play's backers.

The Chalk Garden, with settings and costumes by Cecil Beaton, was regarded by many of the new-wave directors as in the out-moded tradition of the English drawing-room piece in three acts, with one set and a French window at the rear leading to the chalk garden. The plot centres on Miss Madrigal (Siobhán) who is hired as a governess for a problem child, the granddaughter of the rather scatty razor-tongued lady of a Sussex manor (Gladys Cooper).

"The best part," quipped Siobhán, "is that of the butler who is never seen but runs the house from his sickbed upstairs." She probably felt, for the first time, that she was straitjacketed by the understated, repressed emotions of this woman with a dubious past. The artificial upper-class style seemed not so much a far cry as a stifled sniffle from the tearing tantrums of Pegeen Mike and the bell-clear voices of Joan of Arc. She told a reporter from the Boston *Sunday Globe*.

> "Frankly, I don't like all those rehearsals in the United States. At the Abbey we worked only two hours a day rehearsing. People asked me how that could be and I explained that we all knew each other so well and our different methods or styles of playing a role that we didn't need any more.
>
> "They didn't work this hard in England because no English actor would consent to Sunday rehearsals. And we rehearse for only half-a-day on Saturday. I was amazed to discover that the day before an opening, actors often rehearse for twelve hours."[30]

Siobhán was clearly unnerved and on edge, as she usually was before an opening. The pre-Broadway try-outs at the Wilbur Theatre, Boston, the Walnut Theatre, Philadelphia, and at New Haven, Connecticut, were nerve-wracking, although the play was well received. There was the inevitable re-writing and the original director, George Cukor, was replaced by Albert Marre after the Boston opening.

"It is a very difficult play. I think the hardest I have ever been in," admitted Siobhán. "It took a long time to get it right. In New Haven, the critics panned it. One of my friends visited me backstage – my friends are brutally frank – and said 'Siobhán, I am shocked, very shocked. Get yourself some TV work right away. It won't last.'"[31]

It did last for nearly six months after the opening night at the Ethel Barrymore Theatre on 26 November 1955. Instead of going to Sardi's to wait up for the notices, Siobhán went back to her apartment to phone Denis in Dublin and tell him that the friend who had told her in New Haven that it would flop had come backstage after the curtain at the Ethel Barrymore to say that she was on a winner. Siobhán was not that sure, as Gladys Cooper had fluffed her way through the first act. Mercifully, the critics didn't notice everything. Walter Kerr wrote:

The company performs brilliantly. Gladys Cooper slams her feet on the floor and bounds from a chair with the authority of a martinet and the winning irrelevance of the eternal chatterbox. Siobhán McKenna sets her faraway eyes on a corner of the future and speaks with simple stunning honesty.[32]

Brooks Atkinson mildly reproved Siobhán in the *New York Times*:

The part of the enigmatic governess is played by a richly talented young Irish actress, Siobhán McKenna, who has a placid look that marks a fiery vitality. She has a habit of raising and lowering the volume of her speech that loses significance for that reason. But her characterisation of a secretive, melancholy but intelligent and forceful woman is a vivid one.[33]

At least he did not mention the Connemara twang or complain like Ken Tynan about the lack of a middle register as if it were her midriff. There are few actors who consistently escape the lash of the more elitist academic critics. Eric Bentley, who once claimed that he never wrote about performances that he did not like, unashamedly contradicted himself in the *New Republic*, although admitting that he saw at least one act twice:

> If first impressions are all, let the management of *The Chalk Garden* take note that I fled the show in dismay after one act ... I walked out the first time because the performance was so full of effort and strain. Gladys Cooper (Mrs St Naughton) was hamming it up, and Siobhán McKenna (Miss Madrigal) would keep pointing her head at the balcony and booming. The performance I saw a couple of months later was a good deal better, though not without the same clumsiness and effortful drive. The vocal quirk must be one Miss McKenna always has trouble with, as it is present in her Juno in the new recording of O'Casey's play; yet my second visit made me see how much the show depends on her un-actressy beauty and strangely fine combination of sturdy and delicate elements.[34]

His comment on the O'Casey play referred to an Angel LP recording of *Juno and the Paycock* with Cyril Cusack as Joxer, Seamus Kavanagh as Captain Boyle and Siobhán as Juno. Generally it is in line with Bentley's poor estimate of ex-Abbey players after his pseudo-Brechtian direction of the Abbey Company in Lorca's *The House of Bernardo Alba* in 1950.

Denis O'Dea, Donnacha and his Irish-speaking governess, Síle Ní Chonchubhair from Ballyferriter, landed in New York from the Queen Mary on 17 November 1955. Denis had been cast as Father O'Malley in Eddie Dowling's off-Broadway production at the Holliday Theatre of *The Righteous Are Bold*. This spiritual shocker, about demonic possession and exorcism in the wilds of Mayo, had a record-breaking run at the Abbey in 1946 with a blood curdling performance by Máire Ní Dhomhnaill as the possessed girl. Unfortunately, the producer Eddie Dowling now entrusted this key role to his ambitious but inexperienced young wife, and the play folded after a short run. At least it brought the O'Dea family together again and saved Siobhán from the clutches of the Irish-Americans who seldom go to the theatre but are over-generous hosts to all new arrivals from "the ould sod", as they quaintly call it. Siobhán had been in constant demand for guest appearances at *céilís* and Irish nights in the saloons on Third Avenue. The newshawks were at her heels waiting for a bog-trotter on Broadway to fall into a manhole. One hack on the *Daily News* did little to win friends for Siobhán among the WASPs and socialites of the city:

> Shee-boom (*sic*) believes Ireland will rise again. She says she loves the English, but if I ran Scotland Yard, I'd have Shee-boom's handbag checked regularly for rifles (*sic*), ammo, bombs and sticks of dynamite.
>
> I don't know what she and the old Third Ave goid (pronounced gwid) were talking about when they went into those Gaelic discussions, but I suspect it bodes no good to the Queen.[35]

Such racist garbage landed the exuberant but vulnerable Siobhán in more widely publicised controversy when she became something of a celebrity on television chat shows. Denis, with his old IRA record and exemplary reticence, would never had left himself open to such public-house drivel.

This Irish-speaking theatrical family were top-of-the-bill among the Saint Patrick's Day attractions in 1956. They were front page news on the *New York World Telegram*. On a day which brings out the best and the worst in the American Irish, Siobhán had to be photographed in her bare feet "in a typical Aran Island maid's attire" with a leprechaun journalist rigged-out in a "green pixie-hat, a ruffled, beer-stained shirt-front and a cutaway coat":

> We are freshly come from the prettiest choice of bare toes this side of the Ballyshannon (*sic*) and it pleases us as recalling that there is no scoil to-day. An altogether Irish child put it this way:
>
> "An mbíonn scoil lá pheil (*sic*) Phadraic anseo?"
>
> To which the happy answer is:
>
> "Ní bhionn, buidheachas le Dia."
>
> It was Donnacha (Irish for Denis) who asked about school on St Patrick's Day, and it was Sheila O'Connor, governess and tutor, who said no thanks be! ... Donnacha O'Dea, who is seven and speaks English as well as you or me but only to someone who can't speak Irish ...![36]

Perhaps to do penance, Siobhán appeared on Palm Sunday in a special religious programme on TV in which she read from a translation of Paul Claudel's poem, "*Le Chemin de La Croix*", against a painted backdrop of the Stations of the Cross.

Easter 1956 saw the end of *The Chalk Garden* after a reasonably successful run in a season which was notable for such box-office hits as *Will Success Spoil Rock Hunter?*, with a bosomy Jayne Mansfield; Rex Harrison and Julie Andrews in the stage première of *My Fair Lady*; the Lunts in *The Great Sebastians*; Michael Redgrave in *Tiger at the Gates*; and Nancy Walker in Noel Coward's *Fallen Angels*. In an end-of-season survey *Collier's Magazine* attributed much of the success of *The Chalk Garden* to Siobhán, "an exciting personality with witchery in her voice". She may have been a little disappointed when Katherine Hepburn was cast as Miss Madrigal in the film version, but she wished Peggy Ashcroft well in the part when John Gielgud's West-End production of the play opened in the autumn. Siobhán was still determined to remain in the United States, and play *Saint Joan* there in the centenary year of Shaw's birth.

Denis and Donnacha went home. Denis played occasional supporting roles in films and in BBC television and Donnacha resumed his schooling at Scoil Lorcán and later at the school around the corner, the Christian Brothers, Synge Street. Siobhán had grown tired of the uncomfortable Georgian grandeur of the house in South Richmond Street and urged Denis to buy a farm as an investment for retirement – "about forty acres, horses, and a few cows and bullocks to pay for the bets on the horses". Denis bought her down to earth when he asked her how she would like to get up in the middle of the night when a cow was calving. She believed then that Denis would outlive her, but, if this were to happen, Denis would prefer to do so in his old home in South Richmond Street. He loved to go to the west of Ireland on fishing trips or for a few days at the races, but home was always Dublin and the all-night poker games at the Royal Marine Hotel, Dun Laoghaire, or the Dolphin Hotel where they sometimes played through Saturday night and Sunday morning until it was time for Father "Flash" Kavanagh's 1.00 p.m. mass at St Audeon's. Big gamblers can be deeply religious, and I heard one high roller say of another punter who had given up going to mass: "He never had a day's luck afterwards – not even at the dogs!" This was a precarious winner-take-all existence which Siobhán did not share. However, it was Denis who was the homebird who looked after Donnacha. From an early age, Denis encouraged his son to practise swimming seriously until in a few years he was the best of his generation. As Denis said when Donnacha was twelve times Irish champion: "He has beaten all the old men in Ireland except myself."

Notes

1. George Bernard Shaw, Preface to *St Joan* (Penguin, 1954) p.38
2. Liam Mac Gabhann, interview with Siobhán McKenna, *The People*, 5 August 1956
3. Ibid.
4. Ibid.
5. Ibid.
6. *The People*, 5 August 1956
7. *Evening Mail*, 12 January 1951
8. Des Hickey and Gus Smith, *A Paler Shade of Green* (Leslie Frewin, 1972) pp.53-54
9. *Jubilee*, October 1956, p.26
10. Extract from an unpublished autobiography of Shelah Richards, compiled by Robert Hogan from her notes and recordings made by him in 1982-83.
11. "Cruiskeen Lawn," *Irish Times*, 24 June 1951
12. Letter to Denis O'Dea from 37 Nottingham Place, London, 1 April 1953
13. Ibid.
14. *Letters of Sean O'Casey*, Vol. II (Macmillan) p.967
15. Letter from Sean O'Casey to Siobhán McKenna, 16 June 1953
16. Undated letter from Siobhán to Denis O'Dea from The Grand Theatre, Blackpool
17. Jordan R. Young, *The Beckett Actor: Jack McGowran* (Moonstone Press, 1957) p.40
18. Des Hickey and Gus Smith, *A Paler Shade of Green*.
19. *The People*, 5 August 1956
20. Bernard Shaw, *Collected Letters 1926-1950* (Max Reinhardt, 1983) p.493
21. Letter from Patrick O'Reilly to Mrs. O'Dea (*sic*), November 1953. If the photograph was taken, it has not yet been traced.
22. Siobhán McKenna, "GBS, A Centenary Bouquet," Chrysalis, Vol. IX (1956) pp.10-11
23. Harold Hobson, *Sunday Times*, 3 October 1954
24. Ibid.
25. Kenneth Tynan, *Curtains*, p.83
26. John Barber, *Daily Express*, 30 September 1954
27. Stephen Williams, *Evening News*, 30 September 1954
28. Siobhán McKenna, "GBS, A Centenary Bouquet," pp.10-11
29. *The Kenneth William Diaries* (HarperCollins, 1993)
30. Quoted by Marjory Adams, Boston *Sunday Globe*, 25 September 1955
31. Helen Duker, interview with Siobhán McKenna, *New York Post*, 27 November 1955
32. Walter Kerr, New York *Herald Tribune*, 27 November 1955

33. Brooks Atkinson, *New York Times*, 27 November 1955
34. *New Republic*, 26 March 1956
35. Charles McHarry, *Daily News*, 14 September 1955
36. John M. McGuire, *New York World Telegram*, 17 March 1956

In Full Flight

S IOBHÁN ONCE INTRODUCED me to William Morris (Bill) Hunt, a
distinguished-looking Bostonian, as "the man who gave me my
first chance to play Saint Joan in the States". This dignified
patrician had been one of the promoters of the Cambridge Drama
Festival, during which the play was presented at the Saunders
Theatre on 16 August 1956. Hunt was to become a life-long friend,
together with another of the promoters, Michael (Mandy) Wager,
who played the Dauphin in that production. There had been misgivings on the part of some patrons about the inclusion of the play,
mainly because there had been a semi-professional production a
month earlier at the Theatre on the Green at Wellesley College,
which featured a Saint Joan with the unpromising name of Nancy
Wickwire. It appears to have been a ramshackle affair in which the
five scenes were played without an interval and with five or six
wooden benches as the only properties.

Now that the more informed theatregoers could pronounce her
first name, Siobhán, probably jocosely, told columnists that it really
should be *Sidhe-Bhán* or White Spirit. Her impish sense of fun made
it natural for her to play the Irish card. Fortunately, there was no
Irish stampede to shift America's acclaimed Joans – Winifred Lenihan,
Katharine Cornell, Uta Hagen and Julie Harris – off their pedestals.
The Irish-Americans, most numerous in South Boston, seldom
ventured across the Charles River to Cambridge and certainly not to

see a play; so it would be all the greater triumph for Siobhán if the Brahmins came to cheer. Siobhán was quietly confident with Albert Marre again as her director and an ancient Abbey actor, P.J. Kelly, in the small part of the steward, to bring her luck. The *Boston Globe* headline – "Irish Saint Joan is Superb" – led the salvoes of praise:

Acclaimed by the British public and press as the finest Shavian Saint Joan of this generation and idolised in her native Ireland for the same role, Siobhán McKenna of the golden rich voice and the superb talent presented her Joan at the Cambridge Drama Festival in Saunders Theatre last night. The characterisation is magnificent.

It is a peasant girl – with bare feet – who makes her first entrance in that unforgettable scene with Robert de Baudricourt. It is a wan, sorrow-ridden young woman who goes to the stake – but she possesses a grandeur and a greatness that fills the theatre with emotion.[1]

The highly influential Elliot Norton in a notice, "Second Thoughts of a First Night", threw caution to the wings of the stage:

Siobhán McKenna is the greatest Joan of our generation, and on the basis of this performance, one of the greatest living actresses.

Short, straight, and sturdy with a crown of jet-black hair cut after the fashion of the mediaeval soldier, she is no beauty. Her face is broad, her features unimpressive. But her Joan is a blazing figure of radiant innocence, vital force and a driving spiritual intensity. She takes hold of the imagination and the emotions on her first rushing entrance and never lets go. From that moment, you live in the high and heady air of Joan's presence, exhilarated and exalted.

There has never been and probably never will be a Joan of such vitality and such variety. The soul of the saint burns in this girl's performance, a fierce flame in the high and holy wind of inspiration. She is a new Prometheus, carrying the fire of a spiritual life to a generation that had shivered in cold and stumbled in the darkness. ... Although she is acting with all the art at her command from first to last, Miss McKenna conceals her art and only the living Joan of Arc shines through, an altogether astonishing and unforgettable woman.[2]

The gossip columnist of the *Boston Sunday Post* reported that Archibald McLeish, Arthur L. Loeb, Mrs Winthrop Ames and Mrs

Louise L. Jaffe were so awed that they saw the play more than once. But even after repeating her triumph in the Theatre in the Park in Philadelphia, it seemed that a Broadway première would again prove difficult. There were some, apart from Julie Harris fans, who thought of Siobhán's Joan, to quote Shaw, "as the queerest fish among the eccentric worthies of the Middle Ages". Despite critical fanfares in Boston and Philadelphia, the play only sneaked into the downtown off-Broadway Phoenix Theatre in mid-September. There had been demands for replacements of a few actors whose performances the management thought inadequate. With a sense of loyalty and self-confidence, Siobhán demurred: "When I think of what being replaced does to an actor, I feel that no show is worth the damage."[3] The play opened with the original cast.

Brooks Atkinson, who was uneasy at her London performance, was still shifty in his seat in the stalls:

> Doubtless this is the most vigorous performance Shaw's Joan ever had. Miss McKenna fairly bursts into every scene, and usually at the top of her voice. She reads her lines with a sing-song rhythm that becomes rather hypnotic before the play is over. But the accent is Irish, which makes it particularly attractive to American ears, and the voice is extraordinarily powerful.
>
> There's more to Shaw's Joan than the peasant-girl. As the title proves, there is the saint. It was the spiritual mystery of Joan that attracted Shaw to her as a subject for his finest work. Miss McKenna does not bring much illumination to the spiritual aspects of this thoughtful, enquiring study in the realm of faith.[4]

Brooks Atkinson rated Albert Marre's direction and staging "superior to the one that took London by storm in 1955",[5] but he left readers in no doubt of his view that quite a lot of Shaw was "neither felt nor communicated in Miss McKenna's acting".

John Beauford in the *Christian Science Monitor* commented that

> the curious deliberation of Miss McKenna's delivery, plus her tendency to stress unimportant words, mars the rhythm and beauty of the text. The drama and tragedy of Joan suffer, and some of the rich music is lost, when the lines are misspoken.[6]

It seemed unlikely that with such poor notices the production would run and transfer to another theatre. Her best friends hoped that Siobhán was not romancing when she said she never read first night reviews. Those who had seen her play the part in Dublin and London refused to accept that her characterisation had suffered a sea-change on its journey across the Atlantic. Brooks Atkinson's use of the derogatory word "vigorous" recalled Shaw's story of the fiddler who, when asked whether he played by ear or by note, answered, "Be neither but be main strength."

It is most likely that Richard Watt Jr's notice in the *New York Post* came to the play's rescue:

> The new presentation of Shaw's finest drama ... is an admirable one in every way and the quality of what can be called without a moment of hesitation a masterpiece comes through with inescapable force and magnificence. Happily *Saint Joan* has not been done as merely a starring vehicle for an exceptional actress. But it is also true that Miss McKenna seems to give the play a new quality of incandescence, and that is because we have never seen the role portrayed with such deeply instinctive feeling for it.
>
> To appreciate the spiritual triumph of Joan completely, it is necessary to believe in the actuality of her voices, in her calm confidence in herself in the midst of defeat and disaster and in her ability to impress her qualities of leadership and spiritual strength on even the sceptical and resentful men about her. I think Miss McKenna manages all these things with remarkable simplicity and utter conviction, and the peasant girl who was a warrior, saint and poet comes to complete life![7]

The very qualities which Watts admired in her performance were sorely needed by Siobhán personally if she were to withstand the critical stabs of the dreaded butchers of Broadway. The audience response was excellent and several letters appeared in the *New York Times* deploring Brooks Atkinson's dismissive notice. After ninety-three performances at the Phoenix Theatre, the play transferred to the Coronet Theatre, under the management of Roger L. Stevens and Jermee Friedman, where it opened for a matinée performance on Christmas Day 1956, with eight changes of cast. Alexander Scourby was now the Bishop of Beauvais and Tom Clancy, better known as one of the Clancy Brothers, the famous balladeers from Carrick-on-Suir, appeared as Captain Le Hire. The run at the Coronet was a "hot ticket" at the box-office but was limited by an Equity restriction that "alien" (non-American) actors could not be engaged for more than six months in any one New York production.

This would not normally have concerned Siobhán but she applied for an extension of the Equity license in this instance, on the grounds that at her age "she was getting long in the jaw for the part of the maid. I shall never dare to hobble on in the part after this year."

A matinée on Christmas Day was a perilous date for an Irish actor to open on Broadway. Close friends told Siobhán to keep away from the non-stop receptions and parties and to steer clear of the more tasteless publicity stunts, some of which were more appropriate to the post-Boucicault era of Irish melodrama. A well-meaning friend, Kruger Kavanagh from Dunquin, who had once worked as a publicity man for the impresario and composer Victor Herbert and tenor Walter Scanlon, wrote to Milton Shubert telling him how to sell Siobhán on Broadway. For publicity, Kruger suggested that three large blow-ups of Siobhán's portrait be mounted in the frame of a giant shamrock over the theatre entrance so that Irish Americans would rush the box-office, even on Christmas Day. "That's how we did it," said Kruger, "for *Abie's Irish Rose*." Although she avoided such shamrockery or shamroguery, Siobhán did herself some harm when she agreed to appear on Mike Wallace's TV chat show *Night Beat*, for which she was obviously unprepared.

Earlier that year, had Siobhán co-starred in several spectacular NBC television adaptations of successful works of an earlier era. She was now known to millions of television viewers from coast to coast after appearing in *The Letter* by Somerset Maugham with John Mills, and *Cradle Song* by the Sierra Brothers with Judith Anderson. In the television version of *The Letter* she was billed as "the great new star of the Broadway stage" and directed by William Wyler, who had won an Academy Award for his direction of Bette Davis in the same part in the motion picture of the same novel.

It is likely that Siobhán expected her television host to ask her about her past triumphs and expectations for the future, but Mike Wallace was one of the early exponents on television of the kind of bruising cross-examination people flinch from in a court of law. She soon found herself facing, under remorseless close-up, the modern equivalent of Shaw's Inquisitor. Wallace wanted to know why she personally believed in miracles and was clearly not prepared to listen to any blarney about her "voices", so preventing her from getting in a plug for the show. Next, Wallace enquired, "Why is Ireland's birth rate so low?" Siobhán mumbled, "It's a poor country." When the compère quoted Tyrone Guthrie as saying that the Irish theatre was moribund, Siobhán smiled tolerantly and told him, "Tyrone is from the North of Ireland." She failed to interest Wallace in what was her own birthplace, and he wanted to know more about Robert Briscoe, the Jewish Lord Mayor of Dublin. "He's an Irishman," explained Siobhán. Not interested in national sentiment, Wallace asked if there was a large Jewish community in Dublin.

"Yes," she replied, and added irrelevantly, "not anywhere else in Ireland, but in Cork and Dublin there are." She agreed that the Jews did well in business. "It's also to our advantage because, for instance, Guinness's Brewery. Mr Guinness is Jewish and he employs thousands and thousands of Dublin people, and gives them wondeful business and all that. Of course it is good."

It was not good. One can only wonder what the Guinness peer, Lord Moyne, who gave the Rupert Guinness Hall to the Abbey Theatre when they were homeless after the fire, thought of such baloney. Live late-night television was obviously not Siobhán's *métier*. Bravely she came back on the show the following night to try to explain to those who had phoned in accusing her of anti-semitism.

"I am about as anti-semitic as the Chief Rabbi of Israel, who was born in Dublin." She was clearly distressed. "I am quite shocked to learn that what I said not only hurt some people but it was thought that these remarks by me were meant as an insult to the Jewish people ... I am sorry if I have hurt anyone inadvertently, but I think it's just because I didn't express myself well."[8]

She was deeply hurt when twenty-three years later Conor Cruise O'Brien, the editor-in-chief of the *Observer*, in an article "On Being A Jewish Wild Goose", about Jews and Irish Catholics in general not mixing very well, made much of Siobhán's indiscretion:

The neighbourhood of Ireland and Israel, in the context of Jewish and Irish Manhattan, sometimes produces strange crackles. One night Miss Siobhán McKenna, the gifted and patriotic Irish actress, was interviewed on television. The interviewer was one of those grasshopper types who speedily get tired of the subject on which the interviewee can speak with authority – in this case the stage – and move on to something else, in the hope of God knows what. The interviewer wanted to discuss economics, a subject to which Miss McKenna favoured the intuitive approach.

"How is the Irish economy doing, Miss McKenna?"

"Terrible, awful, unspeakable, ruin."

"Really, Miss McKenna, and how do you account for that?"

"The Jews," said Miss McKenna crisply, spang (*sic*) into the CBS camera.

The towers of Manhattan crackled and re-formed in the violet air. The Jews had taken all the Irish money.[9]

Siobhán, obviously not at her best, had given some silly and scatterbrained replies but she hardly deserved such a roasting in the lofty columns of the *Observer*. She was, in 1979, a member of the Council of State and no longer an *ingénue* of Broadway. She sued the *Observer* for defamation on the grounds that the article accused her of anti-semitism, but when the original transcript of the broadcast was made available to the *Observer* she dropped the case. Conor Cruise O'Brien properly withdrew the allegation that she was anti-semitic.[10]

Her new friend, Michael (Mandy) Wager was a son of ·Meyer Weisgel of the Weitzman Institute of Science in Israel. Moreover, Denis and Siobhán were always on friendly terms with such well-known Dublin Jewish families as the Ellimans, the Wines and the Briscoes. Perhaps to make amends for her television gaffe, she appeared with Dublin's Lord Mayor, Robert Briscoe, on NBC's radio Passover performance "The Eternal Light", made in co-operation with the Jewish Theological Seminary in June 1957.

There were other disquieting signs of a lack of her customary professionalism during the short run at the Coronet Theatre when on New Year's Day 1957 she turned up an hour late for the matinée. The audience were about to be given pass-outs when she arrived backstage at about 3:25 pm and they were recalled to their seats: "The Irish star, going directly to her dressing room to prepare for the role, offered no explanation for her tardiness," said one reporter. Another ran the story, "Saint Joan's voices failed her on New Year's Day and so did the alarm clock."

Another television appearance on Ed Morrow's network show *Small World* saw Siobhán cross swords with the ice-cool Noel Coward. It was an international hook-up, with Noel Coward in Jamaica, Siobhán in Dublin and James Thurber in New York. The subject for discussion was supposed to be "humour", but early in the proceedings it sounded more like bad humour. Coward goaded Siobhán by telling her that he liked the Irish but that they were very unreliable, like veal.

"Like what?" asked Siobhán.

He repeated: "Veal."

"Sorry, Noel, I can't hear you," said Siobhán apologetically.

"Veal," he repeated, making it sound even more disgusting.

They could not hear one another very well which made Siobhán even more annoyed, so she roared with ironic laughter. He then said that there were thugs and corner-boys among the Irish who delighted in blowing-up little old ladies posting letters in English letter-boxes.

"I'm afraid he got it from me, then," added Siobhán. "I told him I knew of no little old ladies who had been blown-up and that those he called thugs and corner boys were idealists, many of them teachers. There was a furore from the Stormont Government and questions in the House of Commons. Lord Brookeborough, the Stormont Prime Minister, said he would like to put me across his knee and spank me."[11]

Thurber, the wise old owl, kept out of it. Coward mentioned briefly in his diaries that Siobhán was "wonderful".[12] Certainly no actress, with the possible exception of Vanessa Redgrave, could cause such a stir among the politicians with her off-the-cuff remarks.

"Angels and Ministers of Grace Defend Us" was a headline to which the more blasé of New York theatregoers said "Amen" when, in the last week of January 1957, it was announced that Siobhán McKenna would "go it alone" as Hamlet in the Theatre de Lys in Greenwich Village. The New York Chapter of the American National Theatre had been formed to present "plays of substance, using the finest performers available; to experiment in new forms and techniques; and to hold concert-readings of works too elaborate for full-scale Broadway productions ... production details are emphasised to put emphasis on the actor and the play itself."[13]

The emphasis was certainly on Siobhán more than on the play when the director, Henry Hewes, planned that Siobhán, wearing doublet and hose and other princely accoutrements, should appear alone on the stage in this "experimental" version of *Hamlet*. The other characters, heard only as disembodied voices from the wings, included such old friends as Michael (Mandy) Wager as Horatio and Tom Clancy as Laertes. Joyce Eberts's vocal contribution as Ophelia left one caustic

critic wondering "what Minnie Mouse was doing these days".
Siobhán's ambition to play Hamlet solo was described as

a noble manifestation of the drive which once impelled ladies to fight tooth and nail for the vote, the cigarette smoked in public, and the martini hoisted openly at the bar ... This version of the tragedy of the Prince of Denmark is strictly a stunt, if you'll pardon a little plain speaking ... Gertrude, Claudius and the rest of the folks around the castle are thus no more corporeal than those of Hamlet's father.[14]

Critic Brooks Atkinson turned up like a spectre at the self-indulgent feast. He wanted to know:

How do theatre people get into these cultural jams? Here is Siobhán McKenna with Saint Joan firmly in her bag, now switching sexes and reciting two hours of Hamlet's part ... Hamlet has been played by enterprising women before, though the custom is not recommended here ... Hamlet is a formidable part in a myriad minded play. There is nothing in Miss McKenna's performance nor Mr Hewes's "experimental production" that recognises the stature of the play or the passion and poetry of Shakespeare.[15]

No doubt such comments would be dismissed nowadays, when sex-change on stage is old hat, as dire examples of male chauvinism. There were also problems with the actors "behind the arras" that worried more than Polonius. Siobhán's friend, Mandy Wager, as an unseen Horatio, was "so eaten-up with jealousy that he had to go into analysis".[16]

Siobhán was probably satisfied that she had humbly followed in the footsteps of the great Sarah Bernhardt whose Hamlet was, to quote Maurice Baring, "a marvel, a tiger, natural, easy, lifelike and princely". I once asked Siobhán why we had never seen her Hamlet at home. "I don't think Dublin is quite ready for it," she said dryly.

Even after the *Hamlet* debacle, the newshawks were promising New York that next season they would see Siobhán in yet another version of *Waiting for Godot*, in which she would play all the principal roles. She was a woman of infinite jest who was always "good for a quote" in the gossip columns. Wisely, she decided to quit the fooling and to do some real Shakespeare for a change.

Despite Siobhán's public disapproval of his views on the Irish theatre, she was glad to accept Tyrone Guthrie's invitation to play Viola in *Twelfth Night* at the Stratford Shakespearean Festival in Ontario. Guthrie liked her Saint Joan immensely, preferring it to Sybil Thorndike's first English performance:

> Thorndike, in a raucous Lancashire accent, violently smacking all the other actors on the back and shoulders, violently smacking her own knees and even her own behind, was the New Girl's nightmare about the Games Mistress. Also, even in 1924, she was a tiny bit too old![17]

If Siobhán expected any special favours from Tyrone Guthrie, she got a rude awakening when she arrived late for rehearsal on her first day at the Stratford Ontario Theatre. The new festival theatre was still in the course of completion and nobody had told Siobhán that a cold and draughty dancehall was where rehearsals were taking place. A cast clad in windbreakers and heavy sweaters awaited the arrival of the guest celebrity. When Siobhán arrived at last, Guthrie, scarcely listening to Siobhán's mumbled apologies, clapped his hands and witheringly announced: "Now that the star has arrived, perhaps we can begin!"

Siobhán flared: "Don't you dare to call me a star!" Sensing the start of a shindig, the rest of the cast retreated further into the folds of their winterwear. Word had got around that Siobhán did not really want to play Viola at all and that her first choice was Cleopatra. But the festival directors had insisted on a comedy to balance the second play of the season, *Hamlet*, starring Christopher Plummer. After the unpleasant exchange of greetings, Siobhán got a further jolt when Guthrie announced that Shakespeare's comedies were no laughing matter and that they would underline the melancholy aspect of *Twelfth Night* because everybody in the cast, except Fabian and Maria, were "quite mad". Siobhán, cold and ashen-faced, could scarcely believe her ears. She had looked forward to high-jinks in the tomboyish scenes, at least, when Viola appears disguised as a boy to woo a lady for her master.

After Tyrone Guthrie was satisfied that he had pushed her off her imaginary pedestal, he proceeded to change tactics and to coax a captivating performance from Siobhán right from her opening line, "What country, friend, is this?" At first she bridled against the amount of physical movement and energy Guthrie required of the players. "He literally had us bicycling up a wall," said Siobhán, and when she said she could not cope, he would turn to the others: "Cut it out," he would order with a snap of his long fingers. "You see, she is Abbey. They don't go in for trapeze work." The taunts spurred Siobhán to excel. When the first night reviews appeared, Siobhán shared the honours with Christopher Plummer as Sir Andrew Ague-cheek and Douglas Campbell as Sir Toby Belch. Walter Kerr wrote:

Siobhán McKenna, a radiant Puss-in-Boots in the boyish costume Tanya Moisievitch has designed for her, twists her mouth into a curled-leaf smile, opens her enormous eyes and somehow or other suspends herself in a state of permanent rapture. Miss McKenna's rippling and buttered speech does not always inflect the lines for intelligible emphasis; but it is pitched at a level of silken comedy that keeps the frolic light and the atmosphere heady. The girl is, in this instance, enchanting.[18]

In a Shakespearean part she could not have expected to escape the baleful glare of her Banquo's Ghost, Brooks Atkinson. At least on this occasion she got off lightly, at the expense of Tyrone Guthrie:

This is a *Twelfth Night* that runs to three hours and a quarter, if the two intermissions are included. Having made his points two or three times, Mr Guthrie makes them two or three times more with the same boyish enthusiasm. When the comic mood is on him, Mr Guthrie can never bear to stop. This time he has conspired in long pantomime when Feste is taunting Malvolio in the dungeon. It is fairly unintelligible all the way through; it is also longer than Mr Guthrie, who is the tallest stage director in the Western Hemisphere.[19]

When she read this, Siobhán must have smiled at the irony of these jabs at a director who had announced to his cast that they would not play it for laughs. Brooks Atkinson seemed almost tempted to kiss and make-up with Siobhán:

Miss McKenna is a pleasant Viola. There is something of the stolid Saint Joan peasant in Miss McKenna's Illyrian maiden, which doubtless the author did not foresee, for he was a great toadier of ladies and gentlemen. But Miss McKenna has an exhaustive good humour that is good for the play.[20]

The Stratford Ontario season was a new achievement for Siobhán, but the financial rewards were modest, little more than three hundred dollars per week.

She earned even less during a short summer season at Harvard University where she played opposite Jason Robards in *Macbeth*. The *Time* magazine critic said that "Siobhán made her Lady Macbeth warm and feminine".

"I feel people should have compassion for the sinners of the world," she said.

In her sleepwalking scene, her red hair streamed above a white wispy gown and her hands scrubbed themselves in ghastly compulsion; she put in the greatest mad scene seen in the U.S. since Callas's Lucia de Lammermoor.

Fortunately, she had several offers to appear in new plays by aspiring playwrights with a view to attracting backers for Broadway productions. Actors are notoriously erratic in their judgment of new scripts, frequently mistaking the part for the whole. Siobhán was no better than most and although she had scripts submitted to her from established playwrights like Bridget Boland, she usually deferred a final decision to appear in a play until the last moment.

Occasionally, she relied on intuition, as when she stayed up half the night reading *The Rope Dancers* by television scriptwriter Morton Wisengrad. It dealt with the plight of an Irish-American couple living on New York's Lower East Side at the turn of the century. She told the author the next day that she would do her best to get the Playwrights Company to produce it. A try-out production was planned at the Willow Theatre in Boston, a city which Siobhán found lucky for her. She saw herself in the part of the righteous self-punishing wife and Art Carney was cast as her ne'er-do-well husband. Joan Blondell got the part of the slatternly but good-natured next-door neighbour. Siobhán was particularly pleased that a very young Peter Hall had been invited to make his American debut as director of *The Rope Dancers*.

"Please don't get an American director," Siobhán advised. "They always dramatise *themselves*."

The Boston try-out went well with her local fans and critics, Elliot Norton providing the only dissenting voice:

Groping after some solemn significance, the author has created one remarkable character, the unhappy wife, and has sketched the two others, the father and child. But he hasn't got above the level of a sketch in the latter cases and he doesn't get over the level of soap opera during most of the evening. ... A play of some power might perhaps have been made of this. But this one, except in certain scenes, is static and falsely theatrical, veering away from truth and probability into melodramatic nonsense.[21]

Siobhán, playing the "one remarkable character" referred to above, appeared in New Haven, Newark and Baltimore before the Broadway opening at the Cort Theatre on 20 November 1957. The play had a mixed reception, but Siobhán was hailed as a performer of star quality who could guarantee the success of a run-of-the-mill piece. Walter Kerr in the *Herald Tribune* paid her the enviable tribute that she had succeeded "in playing the unplayable":

In a somewhat more sombre way, *The Rope Dancers* has let itself in for one of those situations. The leading lady, who has blamed her own sex enthusiasm for the deformity that has been inflicted on her only child, decides – in a blind fury – to abandon the false restraints she has built up for years. She rips off her dress, spreads her cloak on the floor, settles down on the cloak, and issues a sneering invitation to her understandably flustered husband. Need I say that the husband discovers he has other things to attend to (not bird watching)? ... I find it impossible to go more thoroughly into the problems of this scene without inviting police action myself, but I think that by now we have formulated the essential question: Should a dramatist ever begin a scene that he has got to get out of before he has written it?[22]

In those pre-*Oh Calcutta* days, this scene was greatly daring, but Siobhán took it in her stride. In the publicity build-up Siobhán went "over the top" in another direction by affirming that the play was so "authentically Irish" that she had decided to play her part in a North of Ireland accent. As if anybody noticed, least of all her *bête noire*, Brooks Atkinson:

In the part of the mother, Siobhán McKenna gives an inspired performance that makes all her previous appearances appear like apprentice work. She is naturally a magnetic actress. There is always a cadence in her voice that is attractive. Everything that she is and knows she has put at the service of this proud but wretched woman whose coldness is really passion, whose poise is really hysteria. It is a sensitive and understanding performance by an artist.[23]

Great actors are frequently remembered for their performances in plays of little worth: Sir Henry Irving in *The Bells*, Sarah Bernhardt in most of the plays which Shaw labelled *Sardoodledom*, Sara Allgood in *Peg O' My Heart*. Now Siobhán in *The Rope Dancers* was the toast of Broadway. She attracted admirers like moths to a flame and, overcoming the tendency of the Irish to stick together when they reach Manhattan, she became the boon companion of such highly sophisticated journalists as Nick Pelaggi and Macklin Milton. A cynical journalist said that she had deserted the Irish mafia for the intellectual mafia of the *New Yorker* and Greenwich Village, where she then had an apartment. The theatre programme publication *Playbill* did not agree in this account of her informal first night parties:

Technically this was more spontaneous hero-worshipping than party. It transpired in Siobhán McKenna's dressing room. The star, who had given one of the most extraordinary performances of the decade, stood, midst floral tributes and well-wishers' telegrams, in a kind of old dressing sack (a garment she wears in the play), her face sweaty and smudgy, like a little girl who had been playing house in the local mud patch. In came all sorts of people. Not many famous people here, but each and every face radiant, as though each person had been drinking in some glorious tribute of nature. Sometimes the dressing room was so thick with brogue that it could have been cut into blocks of peat. Sometimes the dressing room was very, very still, with admirers edging in, pressing the star's hand and gulping with emotion.[24]

This reads like an updated description of an Irish wake. Siobhán fuelled some of this turf-smoke over Manhattan by telling columnists that she was translating *The Rope Dancers* for An Taibhdhearc, but not before she had made a trip to Hollywood to play Mother Cabrini in a film on the life of the first American-born saint, unfortunately not of Irish descent. The Christian Brothers in Synge Street must have feared a transatlantic invasion from the States when she impishly told a reporter:

The kind of school I want for my son is not so much one that struggles to teach him something as one that will make him anxious to know everything.[25]

At her Greenwich Village parties she served colcannon, an Irish recipe, with chablis laced with brandy. She was very much a "fun person" who liked to entertain her less fortunate actor colleagues. When *The Rope Dancers* transferred from the Cort to the Henry Miller Theatre, even the most waspish of the WASP socialites were prepared to admit that Siobhán's acting *tour de force* was the main reason for the play's success. Her innate intelligence would not permit her to admit this as she firmly adhered to the dictum that the play's the thing. She frequently remarked that she was only as good as her last part and knew that her chances of starring in the great classic roles, like Cleopatra, were now strictly limited.

Back home in Dublin, the begrudgers said that the States had spoiled her and begged her to come back. When she did so, in the late nineteen fifties, it was only to be spared the expense of keeping two homes. Denis was working less frequently and was mainly occupied in looking after Donnacha, with the help of Aunt Nancy, and in trying to win a few big pots in the poker schools. Like Siobhán, he was generous with money and often took his impecunious former colleagues for a meal and "a few jars" at the Dolphin. They may not have been really short of money for drink but a good steak was a luxury.

Denis had a name as a practical joker and mimic. Siobhán was once invited to Áras an Uachtaráin by President Eamon de Valera for lunch and Denis did not want to go. Siobhán asked the president if she could bring along her old Abbey friend May Craig instead. De Valera agreed and phoned May Craig to invite her personally. When May picked up the phone to hear De Valera saying, "This is President De Valera", she immediately cut in: "Get off the line, Denis O'Dea. I'd know your voice anywhere!" and banged down the receiver.

Years earlier, Denis's alleged impersonation of Lennox Robinson in Louis D'Alton's comedy *The Money Doesn't Matter* incensed Frank O'Connor who, in a letter to the monthly magazine *The Bell*, accused Denis of guying the distinguished Abbey director and playwright as an alcoholic sponger. Denis sued for libel but when it was pointed out to him that *The Bell*, like most literary magazines, had no money in the kitty, like a good poker player he threw in his cards, settling for an apology and nominal damages. Another of his pranks took place on the first night of Myles na Gopaleen's *Faustus Kelly*. The author (Brian O'Nolan) would not take a curtain call but in response to calls of "Author, Author", Denis went on stage dressed as a pseudonymous Myles na Gopaleen, in knee-breeches, green coat and caubeen, wielding a shillelagh.

All this hilarity did not lessen Siobhán's respect for Denis as a father-figure of whom she was slightly in awe. As her fame increased, Denis seemed to withdraw from the theatre. He only acted once with the Abbey during their fifteen-year sojourn at the Queen's Theatre, when he returned to play the gravedigger in *The Passing Day* by George Shiels. His Hollywood career – when he appeared with Marilyn Monroe in *Niagara* and Grace Kelly in *Mogambo* – was soon forgotten.

Siobhán was now a celebrity, who opened charity shows and gave recitals at benefit nights for the needy. She was affectionately but wickedly impersonated as Saint Joan by the comedienne Maureen Potter in Gaiety pantomimes. Only national personalities were chosen for such imitations. She decided to make a new and grander home in Dublin. After the death of his Aunt Josephine, Denis agreed to leave his old home at South Richmond Street to join Siobhán and Donnacha in a more fashionable Victorian-style red-brick residence at 23 Highfield Road, Rathgar.

Notes

1. Marjory Adams, *Boston Sunday Globe*, 17 August 1956
2. Elliot Norton, *Boston Globe,* 20 August, 1956
3. *Saturday Review*, 15 September 1956
4. Brooks Atkinson, *New York Times*, 12 September 1956
5. Ibid.
6. *Christian Science Monitor*, 15 September 1956
7. Richard Watts Jr, *New York Post*, 13 September 1956
8. "On the Air," *New York Times*, 18 December 1956
9. *Observer*, 3 June 1979
10. Phone conversation with Conor Cruise O'Brien, 1 April 1993
11. Gus Smith and Desmond Hickey, *A Paler Shade of Green* p.57
12. Noel Coward, *Diaries* (Weidenfeld & Nicholson, 1982) p.204
13. Programme note, "Theatre de Lys," Spring Season 1957
14. Tom Donnelly, "An Irish Princess from Denmark," *New York Post*, 30 January 1957
15. Brooks Atkinson, "A Distaff Hamlet," *New York Times*, 31 January 1957
16. Interview with Padraic Ó Raghallaigh, RTE, 1983
17. Sir Tyrone Guthrie, *New York Times Magazine*, 27 January 1957

18. Walter Kerr, New York *Herald Tribune*, 4 July 1957
19. Brooks Atkinson, *New York Times*, 4 July 1957
20. Ibid.
21. *Boston Daily Record*, 6 November 1957
22. Walter Kerr, New York *Herald Tribune*, 24 December 1957
23. Brooks Atkinson, *New York Times*, 21 November 1957
24. *Playbill*, 12 December 1957, p.6
25. Jay Camody, "Eire's Drama in America," *The Washington Star*

On the Wing

A FTER THE 1960 Dublin Theatre Festival, its founder, the ebullient impresario Brendan Smith, claimed that it was Europe's biggest drama festival operating on the smallest budget. In that year at the Gaiety Theatre patrons saw MacLiammóir's incomparable evocation of Wilde, *The Importance of Being Oscar*, and Siobhán's reincarnation of her Pegeen Mike in a new production of *The Playboy*, once again directed by her old friend Shelah Richards, in settings designed by the well-known artist Patrick Scott. Never before in its long history had the Gaiety seen such spine-tingling performances in successive weeks.

James Agate had written that whoever saw Máire O'Neill, in the springtime of her career, create the part of Pegeen Mike knew that it would never be played as well again. As one who saw Máire O'Neill in the autumn of her career, when I worked with her in a radio production of *Riders to the Sea*, I never doubted that there could be a second spring. Siobhán's performances in earlier productions had the stamp of greatness; but now she added the poetry of balletic movement to the rich harmonies of her voice. It is here that one must part company with Agate in his belief that Synge's beloved Máire O'Neill gave theatregoers the definitive Pegeen. Mary Frances McHugh, the novelist, who was probably our first woman drama critic, wrote to tell Siobhán that her Pegeen Mike was "the finest she had ever seen".[1] Although Máire O'Neill had been coached by

Synge, there was more of Ballybough than Belmullet in her accent. Seamus Kelly, the *Irish Times* critic, could never make up his mind between Ann Clery and Bríd Ní Loingsigh in the part. Perhaps there never was and never will be a definitive Pegeen; she re-invents herself in every generation to bewitch the Christy Mahons anew.

Siobhán's new Christy was the youthful Donal Donnelly, who brought agility and a seemingly natural innocence to the part. Shelah Richards and Siobhán had too much respect for the integrity of Synge's text to attempt anything shocking or revolutionary. Nor would they have been satisfied with a Christy who would do little more than feed Pegeen with well-timed cues for her impassioned speeches. With forgiveable forgetfulness that she was now thirty-eight, Siobhán had decided that Christy Mahons like the old maestro Cyril Cusack were now too long in the tooth for those love bites. Eithne Dunne, who had years earlier played Pegeen on Broadway opposite Burgess Meredith, brought a Spanish elegance to her interpretation of the Widow Quin, taking the stage "bedecked and bedizened like Pharaoh's Ma".

Internationally, Miss McKenna, as she was formally known, now shared a queen's privilege to be known by her lovely first name, but few could have expected that Harold Hobson would become her poet laureate on her appearance at the Piccadilly Theatre, London, on 12 October 1960. Hailing the production as final and definitive, Hobson chirruped:

It is the Mona Lisa and the Tower of Pisa,
It's the nimble tread
Of the feet of Fred
Astaire.
It's Camembert![2]

Henry Sherek, who co-produced with Brendan Smith, brought a little extra drama to the first night by scrapping the free list for social celebrities and making all seats, except those for the press, available only through the box-office. "The audience," reported *Punch*, "was noticeably more intelligent and there were fewer foyer-crawlers waiting ten minutes after curtain time to be photographed in their latest dresses."[3]

Harold Hobson mentioned that in the early scenes of the play, although Pegeen was making:

sounds of haunting beauty, the audience could hardly understand a word she was saying ... she properly throughout the evening made no concessions. She had determined to show that human speech is unbounded by the restrictions of English phonetics: and show us she did. Not for her the ambition to speak like a duchess or a shop girl in the best emporia; in her view, the proper place for Professor Higgins would have been back at night school.[4]

Siobhán had an unfilled ambition to play Eliza in *Pygmalion* as

a character more tragic than Juno ... Whatever happens, Juno can look after herself. But after Professor Higgins had finished with her, Eliza is helpless ... neither fish, flesh or good red herring.[5]

Under the stage-Irish heading "What Gabble Bedad!" Bernard Levin seemed preoccupied with an off-stage performance. It was not the Synge-song alone that distracted him:

The effect was spoiled for the next ten minutes or so by the fact that nothing could be heard from where I was sitting but an altercation between an usherette and a couple she was accusing of being not merely in the wrong seats but in the wrong theatre.

The great cry that rang out from the dress play circle at the first night of Mr Dominic Behan's play [*Posterity Be Damned*] last March – "Isn't there a single man sober in the whole of Ireland?" expressed the feelings of all of us when faced with the torrent of words that flows across the footlights whenever an Irish playwright takes to the boards.[6]

However, Siobhán swam against the torrent. Bernard Levin enthused:

Miss McKenna touches her words and they burst into flame. She tosses her head and the stars dance. She wrings indignation from a look, love from a gasp, and infinite ravishing beauty from every syllable she utters.

It is the kind of performance that comes once, and not again, and nothing short of damnation will suffice for those who miss it.[7]

Kenneth Tynan had been widely quoted when a few years earlier in a review of Brendan Behan's *The Quare Fellow* he wrote:

It is Ireland's sacred duty to send over every few years a

playwright who will save the English theatre from inarticulate dumbness. And Irish dialogue almost invariably sparkles.[8]

Now he seemed intent on doing a dissection job on a long-dead Irish playwright using not only a scalpel but a stiletto:

The Playboy of the Western World (Piccadilly) is excellent company once in a while but it is possible to have too much of a good Synge. In the past four years, I have seen the play five times, including the musical comedy version [*The Heart's a Wonder* by Nuala and Maureen O'Farrell] and the one presented by the Berliner Ensemble who changed the title to *The Hero of the Western World* and linked Christy Mahon's Ireland to Mike Hammer's America by means of a front cloth covered with Mickey Spillane's dust-jackets (Message: in decadent societies murderers are idolised).

In short I have had a basinful of Synge's sorcery; and for this reason I smile less readily than I once did at his quips about Irish parents, Irish tippling, Irish priests and Irish braggerty ... Even the style is beginning to defeat me. I concede its soft lyricism; but where is its hard meaning? Synge is often praised for his mastery of cadence and for the splendours of his dying falls. Dying they may well be, but they take an unconscionable time doing so. Synge seldom lets a simple, decorative sentence alone. To its tail must be pinned some such trailing tin-can of verbiage, as – to improvise an example – "the way you'd be roaring and boiling in the lug of a Kilkenny ditch, and she with a shift on her would destroy a man entirely, I'm thinking, and him staring till the eyes would be lepping surely from the holes in his head". Nor can I bring myself to devote my full attention to a play in which all the characters are numskulls [*sic*] – and quaint pastoral numskulls at that.

Writers like O'Casey, Behan, J.P. Donleavy [*sic*] have ruined my taste for Synge; and that taste once lost is not easily recovered ... The new production (by Shelah Richards) is full-blooded though slow-paced, with a first-rate Christy from Donal Donnelly and a few embarrassments in minor parts. As Pegeen Mike, Siobhán McKenna gets her arms akimbo and her voice bountifully throbbing. All she lacks is tenderness; instead of a nice girl pretending to be a termagent, she gives us a real termagent.[9]

The play seemed to arouse some racist prejudice, even in the first year of the sixties, in critics like Mervyn John who said that:

The Playboy probably did more than the Phoenix Park murders to prove that the Irish are unfit to govern themselves.[10]

Siobhán herself was often caught in the critical crossfire and seldom ducked for shelter. She could point to the European tour, some weeks earlier, where she was chosen as best actress at the Florence Festival and her illuminating comments on Synge in Berlin:

"We imagined *The Playboy* was a safe play to take to Germany," explained Siobhán, "because it is already popular there in four different adaptations. We knew, therefore, most of the audience would have read it in translation or previously seen it on the Dublin stage. In the case of the classics, previous knowledge of the play adds to one's pleasure and enjoyment. It is not what happens but how it happens that counts – and the more you know about the play, the more you enjoy it.

"While in Berlin, Helene Weigel, Brecht's widow, invited us to see the Berliner Ensemble perform *The Playboy*, her husband's last production before he died. We crossed over to East Berlin and were fascinated by the conception of the play. It was treated as a joke which means that the first act was magnificent but that the guts were taken out of the other two because they were played prosaically and lacked poetry. The final curtain was strangely unmoving.

"The title was meant to mean 'The Corruption of the Western World' and an ingeniously designed act-drop clearly indicated that the Western World loved murder ... In *The Playboy* it is the poetry that carries the emotion. In most other plays the reverse is the case. If you obey Synge's specified rhythms, the emotion rings true, but not a single comma, semi-colon or full stop must be ignored. There are certain phrases intended to be taken in one breath. If the actor splits them, some of the excitement is inevitably lost. There is far more playing in a Synge role than an audience expects and above all, it must look easy. Timing, of course, is of paramount importance."[11]

Siobhán's comments on Synge were strictly in the purist Abbey tradition. Lennox Robinson, making fun of those who could not pronounce the playwright's name correctly, used to say, "You singe a cat, you sing Synge."

Siobhán liked to think that Shelah Richards and herself had assembled a cast that could match the performance of Máire

O'Neill, Fred O'Donovan, Sara Allgood and Arthur Sinclair. The Irish classics, she believed, were best performed by an all-Irish company because their team-work seemed to differ from that of other players. She had become tired of hearing O'Casey and Synge played with New York accents. She summed up:

> "I think British audiences find the lines even more difficult to understand when they are spoken by actors putting-on an Irish accent. Audiences at the Piccadilly are not missing any of the laughs, which seems to confirm that the spirit of the play is getting across. They may be puzzled by certain Gaelic expressions, just as they are by certain Elizabethan phrases in Shakespeare, but anyone who listens can understand. In some curious way they sense the meaning."[12]

Few Irish actresses apart from Siobhán had bothered to comment on their approach to acting. One of the first Abbey company, Máire Nic Shuibhlaigh, wrote:

> At first I found Synge's lines almost impossible to deliver ... like the wandering ballad-singer I had to "humour" them into a strange tune, changing the metre several times each minute ... It is most difficult for an actor to master.[13]

The secret of playing Synge, according to Siobhán, could be summed up in Frank Fay's direction to his players that they should be the *mouthpiece* of their character rather than the character. There is a subtle distinction here which complements Fay's dictum that the sound is part of the meaning.

Artistic achievement never paid golden dividends for Siobhán; the financial rewards had not been great since her early foray into films, which had been deservedly forgotten. She had decided that she would never make another film. "The directors," she said, "made me feel like a pawn on a chess-board." But when Zeffirelli offered her the part of the Virgin Mary in his eight million-dollar production of *King of Kings*, she overcame her initial misgivings and set off for Spain with her twelve-year-old son Donnacha. He was considered for the non-speaking part of the young Jesus but the casting director decided that he did not resemble the star, Jeffrey Hunter, who was to play Christ. A publicity sheet, *The Star* – named after the Star of Bethlehem – tried to give a whiff of incense to this piece of commercial religiosity. Siobhán herself took a swing of the thurible.

"When I was first approached about playing the Virgin Mary, I felt that it was a very dangerous role for any actress to take on; that, indeed, it should not be played. But when I read the script, I was completely overcome.

"It had originally been written by a Christian," she naively added, not disclosing whether it was Matthew, Mark, Luke or John. "Then they got a non-Christian, a Jew, to write it, and I think it has marvellous purity.

"People have been very sarcastic about the film because an actor who had been previously associated with cowboy pictures was playing Christ. But I think that Jeffrey Hunter has a pair of eyes that are so marvelously sincere everyone is going to be amazed at his performance. Of course, I don't think he'll ever get another cowboy part again."[14]

At least she was right about that. No sooner was she back from Spain than she was in discussion with Lord Killanin and Brendan Smith of Four Provinces Productions about making a film of *The Playboy* with an all-Irish cast. "It might not turn out to be box-office," she rightly surmised, "but it should be done ... The important thing is to do it before Hollywood. I don't want some fluffy piece of Hollywood nonsense to make a mess of Pegeen Mike. ... I must play it before Hollywood lays a dead hand on it."[15]

She did play it but not before others, without any help from Hollywood, unwittingly laid a dead hand on it.

Ever since Clark Gable refused to wear a beard in the part of Parnell, miscasting in "Irish" films or in films on Irish subjects has been a by-word in theatre circles. Admittedly there has been an improvement in recent years but the casting of the Irish-born Richard Harris in *The Field* only goes to prove that there is no easy solution to this box-office dilemma.

Given Siobhán's enthusiasm for an all-Irish cast, more might have been expected from the production company largely controlled by Brendan Smith and Lord Killanin with a guarantee of Irish government funding. In the early thirties the director Brian Desmond Hurst had filmed Synge's *Riders to the Sea* with Sara Allgood as Maurya, and with the financial backing of Gracie Fields.

Movies, as the experts emphasise, are primarily concerned with images to which words and dialogue must be subordinate. The problem is obvious when it comes to the wild, exuberant aural richness of *The Playboy*. The second commandment in the film-maker's bible is: thou shalt not have strange actors in leading roles. This star-system axiom resulted in the curious casting of a twenty-six-year-old Welshman with box-office good looks as Christy Mahon. His name, Gary Raymond, was only known to film buffs as the actor who had played opposite Richard Burton in the film of John Osborne's *Look Back in Anger*. Although he was thirteen years younger than Siobhán, the age gap did not seem to trouble her. Gary Raymond was her sixth and youngest Playboy. It seemed likely that the director shared the view of some critics that a Welsh accent would be preferable to the unintelligible Synge-song of the Irish contingent. In hindsight, it is hard to understand how Donal Donnelly was scarcely considered. Siobhán may have added to the confusion by naming Eamon Keane, who deputised for Donal Donnelly, as her favourite Playboy. The Kerry actor, who played the part in the Belfast Opera House and at a revival in the Gaiety Theatre, Dublin, had a voice only matched in its richness by a Burton or a MacLiammóir. He was the Playboy to the manner born both on and off the stage, which may have been to his disadvantage in the long run. Gary Raymond, a cross between Marlon Brando as a London teddy-boy and a Dylan Thomas without the poetry, was an apparently unanimous choice. This risky pairing with Siobhán seemed to delight the management in its daring.

The casting of the English actress Elspeth March as the Widow Quin, and the omission of Eithne Dunne, was probably another concession to a more wide-ranging intelligibility. Liam Redmond as Michael James, Niall McGuinness as Old Mahon, Micheál Ó Briain as Shawn Keogh and Brendan Cauldwell as Jimmy Farrell were suitably cast in their severely cut supporting roles.

Perhaps the most notable absentee from the cast list was Denis O'Dea, who had far more film experience than most of the others and who could have played any of the character parts. He had, in fact, played with distinction in an earlier Lord Killanin production, *The Rising of the Moon*. He may not have been interested in what everybody was told was a £100,000 low-budget production in which Siobhán was working for much less than she could earn elsewhere. To a great extent, Denis distanced himself from the project. With his usual reticence, he never gave any reason why, but since the Edinburgh *Playboy* he had never appeared in a play or a film with Siobhán. She merely commented that Denis never really liked the play.

The casting of *The Playboy* was not the only subject of controversy. Somewhere on the Bangor Erris peninsula in Mayo seemed the obvious location. Siobhán would have liked it to have been filmed in Connemara or Mayo but believed Brian Desmond Hurst when he told her that he had travelled one thousand four hundred miles of sea coast in search of a suitable location. Finally he selected Inch on Dingle Bay, surrounded by the Corca Dhuibhne and Iveragh mountain ranges, as a unique backdrop for the happenings in and around Pegeen Mike's shebeen. The wide white strand, backed by sandhills and stretching nearly three miles into the bay, was a natural setting for the "racing, lepping, dancing and the Lord knows what" which, in the play, are described but not seen. Brian Desmond Hurst once said that a young Abbey actor, Eoin Ó Súilleabhaín, son of the author of *Fiche Bliain Ag Fás* (*Twenty Years A-Growing*), had auditioned for the part of Christy and "nearly got it". It was he, according to Hurst, who persuaded the production team that Inch was the place because the Playboy was a Kerryman "reared on wide and windy acres of rich Munster land" somewhere around Mountain Stage, across the sea from Inch where Synge had spent some time during his travels in West Kerry.[16]

Years earlier John Ford's *The Quiet Man*, starring Maureen O'Hara, John Wayne and Barry Fitzgerald, had brought tourists by the thousands to the quiet village of Cong between loughs Corrib and Mask. But apart from some silent films made by the Kalem company in Killarney early in the century and Tom Cooper's homespun tale of the Black and Tan war, *The Dawn*, film-making was still a novelty in Kerry. The Inch *Playboy* with its modest budget could never compete with the megabucks of *Ryan's Daughter* which, eight years later, according to a Dingle wit, "made the idle rich". But in the summer of 1961 *The Playboy* brought excitement and "a good few bob" to Inch and the surrounding area, and many of the locals were employed as extras. Most of the cast stayed in Inch, although the hotel was closed that summer.

The director, Brian Desmond Hurst, lived in a caravan for the five weeks he spent shooting the film. Kate Ashe, who then worked in Foley's pub in Inch, remembers him well because he wore make-up.

"This was a surprise to all of us," she told me, "because very few girls used it in those days, except when they were going to a big dance." Bridie Foley, who still runs the public house at Inch, was delighted that "Siobhán stayed there for five weeks of that summer." She shared a room with Gary Raymond's girlfriend Deline Kidd, whom he married as soon as the film was finished. Mrs Foley believed that some guesthouse keepers were jealous because Siobhán was staying over the pub.

> So pay no attention to what some of the locals will tell you about midnight frolics between Siobhán and Gary Raymond in the sand dunes. That's the usual ould talk. In fact more women than men came to have a look at Siobhán – they even wanted to see what she was having for breakfast ... Denis and Donnacha came down for a fortnight but Denis was never a man for the all-night parties. He spent the rest of the time further west at Kruger's in Dunquin.[17]

While he was in Kruger's Denis, an enthusiastic angler, fished Mount Eagle Lake and Loch Geal on the other side of the Conor Pass. Owing to rheumatism in his arm he found casting with a fly rod difficult and preferred to spin a minnow from the shore or from a boat. Donnacha remembers spending weeks with Denis in a fishing lodge on a remote island on Lough Curreel in the heart of Connemara where they had great catches of white trout.[18]

Denis always enjoyed a stay with Kruger Kavanagh, listening to yarns of his years in the United States when he worked in show business for Victor Herbert, Walter Scanlan and the Shuberts. The dining room in Dunquin was decorated with photographs signed "With Love to Kruger" from stars like Marlene Dietrich, Lillian Gish and Marilyn Monroe. The only unautographed picture in the room was an oleograph of the Sacred Heart over the mantelpiece. Denis is said to have remedied this omission, late one night, by taking the print from its frame and putting it back in its place before morning with the inscription "From Jesus Christ to Kruger".

As filming got underway at Inch Strand the art director for Four Provinces Films had the main electricity lines and poles removed from sight. The coxswain of the Fenit lifeboat was engaged to supervise the extras in the tricky business of launching and beaching *naomhóga* or currachs amid the mighty breakers on the strand. Avril

Box dressed Siobhán's russet tresses between shots while Eileen Gould coached the step-dancers to keep time with Seán Ó Riada's musical score.

A complete cottage, with moveable walls, had been erected on the edge of the beach. During the filming, the chief cameraman Geoffrey Unsworth had the floorboards removed so that he could sink the camera for a low-angle shot. The set was protected from the rain by a giant tarpaulin made specially for the film by the Krupps factory in Essen. For daylight scenes the tarpaulin was rolled back and the curtains drawn on the window to reveal no painted backdrop but a wild and rugged coast.

The director Brian Desmond Hurst also did the screen adaptation, keeping too close to the stage text. Only the love scenes and racecourse scene were filmed outside of what looked like the single stage set for Michael James Flaherty's shebeen.

"The love scenes came so naturally outside," said Siobhán, "that I wondered how I ever played them indoors. ... Pegeen Mike is essentially a lonely person as I see her. There is an aloofness about her. This is particularly evident in the Fair scene.

"She does not mix with the other girls but stands apart watching the Playboy with an ill-concealed look of pride on her face.

"When the race is over, the girls all swarm around him, but his eyes search the crowd for Pegeen Mike! He walks over to her, takes her hand in his and leads her out to dance.

"This is a very tender moment which is missing from the stage production."[19]

Even when the director took his camera out-of-doors, he did not quite escape from the limitations of his simple set. The jockeys on horseback, the tents, the hurdy gurdies and the maggies on the racecourse looked like Jack Yeats cut-outs against a tourist travelogue of the Magillicuddy Reeks and the Stone Age contours of Dingle Bay. Although his cameraman Unsworth filmed the characters against superb backgrounds, they seemed static "mouthpieces" for Synge's torrent of words. The merciless eye of the camera revealed that Pegeen was no longer "a girl that was aged a score", but at least Siobhán had this belated opportunity to let moviegoers see her Pegeen Mike, even if she was too mature in the part.

Irish film buffs seemed faced with another disaster sure to set a native film industry back for another quarter of a century. After the preview in Dublin's Regal Cinema, the knockers were out in force. "Scandal of the Playboy Film" was the *Evening Mail* heading. "Miscasting in Playboy" capped the review in the *Irish Press*. The kindest of the critics could only see Synge's immortals as dim figures in a landscape.

The rumour factory was now busy trying to give Gary Raymond a Galway mother and a gipsy father when what he needed most was a Donal Donnelly or an Eamon Keane to dub his lines. The Four Provinces producers sent Siobhán on a promotional tour to the United States and planned the American première for Boston, where she had always triumphed. For once, the old magic did not work, either in Boston or elsewhere in the States. Robert C. Roman in *Films in Review* reported:

> This unpretentious film version of Synge's great play, adapted and directed by Brian Desmond Hurst, makes plain the deadly effects of a lie and the readiness of men to be deceived. But although Siobhán gives a fine performance as the young woman who wants to believe the blarney the clay-footed, self-styled "Playboy" brings to the peat bogs, she's too old for the part. Synge had Pegeen Mike be a "wild-looking but fine girl of about twenty" and described his youthful protagonist as "a slight young man". Miss McKenna reads the lines as Synge intended, but time has suited her more to the role of the Widow Quin (a do-gooder who does harm).[20]

Newsweek found nothing "cinematically adventurous" in Brian Desmond Hurst's direction but was prepared to accept it as a "celluloid transcript" of the play. The critic had not only an ear for rhythmic speech but a keen eye for bone structure:

> The play is one of the classics of the modern theater. To hear it in the high brogue that marked its cadences in its first performance at the Abbey Theatre, and to watch it with the emphasis of McKenna's exquisite cheekbones and Raymond's long sad jaw is a joy absolute and unbounded.[21]

As an art film it was a failure; nor did it attract the mass audience every movie is expected to win in the States. However, it did help to resurrect a latent prejudice against Synge's play among the descendants of the Irish-Americans who, fifty years earlier, had the Abbey

Theatre cast arrested in Philadelphia for staging an immoral and indecent play. In court, a witness for the prosecution was asked if anything immoral had happened on the stage. Back came the reply, "Not while the curtain was up!"

Some of the American-Irish socialites who had canonised Siobhán as Saint Joan were now ready to exorcise her as a screen Pegeen Mike. She must have thought ruefully of Synge's lines on a woman (Máire O'Neill's sister, Mrs Callender) who disapproved of *The Playboy*:

> Lord, confound this surly sister,
> Blight her brow with blotch and blister,
> Cramp her larynx, lung and liver,
> In her guts, a galling give her.
> Let her live to eat her dinners,
> In Mountjoy with seedy sinners,
> Lord, this judgement quickly bring
> And I'm your servant, J.M. Synge.[22]

Had she consulted her favourite oracle, G.B.S., Siobhán would have been forewarned:

> The arrest of the Irish players is too ordinary to excite comment. All decent people are arrested in the United States – that's why I refuse to go there. Who am I that I should question Philadelphia's right to make itself ridiculous. I warned the Irish players that America being governed by a mysterious race descended probably from one of the lost tribes of Israel, calling themselves American Gaels, are the real Playboys of the Western World.[23]

All through her life, Siobhán's career was inextricably linked with *The Playboy*, either as a player or director. Despite the failure of the film version, she had become entwined with Pegeen Mike as mystically as mistletoe to an oak. And when the time came to use the pruning knife, she lovingly directed others in the part or opted for the part of the brazen, lecherous Widow Quin.

John Arvin Brown invited her to direct the play with an American cast at the Long Wharf Theatre in New Haven, Connecticut, in 1967. She was glad to meet a new challenge. There was a mixed reaction, running the gamut from the fulsome to the sardonic. The *Waterbury Republican* was gushing:

It's never easy to measure just how much a director puts into a play but it is quite obvious that Miss McKenna has poured into the play some of the love and affection she feels for Ireland. ... When the play ends, waves of applause continued until Miss McKenna appeared. At once you realised that there existed true communication between Miss McKenna and the cast as they applauded even louder than the audience.[24]

The *New Haven Register* was having none of this soppy sentimentality:

Unfortunately, what one gets in the Long Wharf production is a self-conscious toughness. ... The blame here must fall to Miss McKenna in making her American directing debut with this production. In her hands, the play meanders unsteadily between moments of roaring – but often meaningless – action and action-less retrospection. In the end, I suppose what is most disturbing is the choice of *The Playboy* itself. Had it been brilliantly done, would it really have more than a passing impact on a contemporary audience?[25]

Ten years later, under Brendan Smith's management, she assembled a company for an Olympia production of *The Playboy* in which she played the Widow Quin. Nearly everybody who played with her, men and women, loved Siobhán and they spoke glowingly of the family atmosphere she tried to create as a director. This bohemian bonhomie could be deceptive: there were times when the Abbey's team-work only existed on stage. Offstage, some of the principal players were hardly on speaking terms and the rest adjourned to the pub across the road to slag the play or the director.

Siobhán used to say, "An Abbey play is a football match and it does not matter who scores the goals." As a director, she unselfishly passed the ball to the younger generation. Her great friend Niall Buggy was cast as the Playboy with Fidelma Cullen from the Abbey playing Pegeen Mike. Great as was their potential, these hugely talented young players must have sensed that they were playing in the shadow of a towering, if not overpowering, Widow Quin. It was inevitable that a review would appear under the heading, "Siobhán a Great Widow in Playboy". It was clear from the *Irish Press* review who was scoring the goals, although the director had an off-day:

Seamus Locke, Siobhán McKenna as Jimín, Brid Ní Loingsigh,
Padraigín Ní Mhaidín in Muireann agus an Phrionnse, *Abbey*
Theatre 1945 (Irish Times)

Denis O'Dea, Siobhán McKenna and Micheál Ó hAonghusa in
Máire Rós, *Abbey Theatre 1948 (Irish Times)*

Siobhán McKenna in Daughter of Darkness, *1949 (Cyril Stanborough)*

Arthur Miller, Marilyn Monroe, Jason Robards and Siobhán McKenna, Harvard 1957

Siobhán McKenna in Saint Joan, *Gate Theatre 1953*

Gladys Cooper and Siobhán McKenna in The Chalk Garden, *New York 1955 (Cecil Beaton)*

Siobhán McKenna and Gary Raymond in The Playboy of the
Western World, *1961 (The Kerryman)*

Denis O'Dea and Marilyn Monroe in Niagara

Siobhán McKenna as Sarah Bernhardt in Memoir, *Dublin Olympia 1977*

Siobhán McKenna as Mommo in Bailegangaire, *Druid Theatre 1985 (Amelia Stein)*

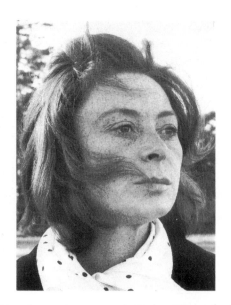

Outdoor photograph (John Hippisley)

The pace is funereal and in several patches borders dangerously on the grave. A slow unfolding should not necessarily march to the tempo of a dead beat.

The Widow Quin in the personage of Siobhán McKenna raises matters considerably and the conflict and the resolution occur with the true spirit of a good wake. Miss McKenna's huge presence provides the vintage from which great performances are savoured. And it is a great performance. This is no conniving widow trying to elicit sexual or domestic favours from Christy Mahon. The Widow Quin is Mother Ireland incarnate, powerful enough to make an Oedipus wretch of men of stronger stuff than whimpering Christy.[26]

Mother Ireland incarnate was a heavy load on her shoulders, but she carried the burden lightly. She toured with the company to the Theatre Royal, Norwich, and then to Hong Kong where the play was welcomed by the ex-pats as light relief in a British colony where there was little or no cultural cross-fertilisation.

Although she could not have foreseen it, *The Playboy of the Western World* was the last movie in which Siobhán played a starring role. The film of Brian Friel's *Philadelphia Here I Come*, in which she played the old housekeeper, was never released on the commercial circuit. She had a supporting part in the unsuccessful 1964 remake of *Of Human Bondage* starring Kim Novak and Laurence Harvey. While fans will remember her in *Doctor Zhivago* (1965), she had only a cameo part in the Pasternak epic. Her earnings from *The Playboy* scarcely exceeded ten thousand pounds inclusive of expenses. But her new home at 23 Highfield Road was elegantly furnished with antiques, many of them purchased on the advice of her friend Monty Marshall, a Jewish dealer. Even when accused of anti-semitism by Conor Cruise O'Brien, Siobhán never opted for the platitude, "Some of my best friends are Jews." She did wryly remark that some of her best friends were "dreadful." But whatever they were like, knowing from experience the vulnerability and insecurity of the actor's calling, she generously paid the bills of those who were down on their luck or who needed help to keep reasonably sober. Although she had a retinue of loyal friends, both male and female, ever ready with advice, she was the person who took the decisions which shaped her career.

It is understandable that the title *Saint Joan of the Stockyards* had an obvious appeal for Siobhán. It was her choice for the Dublin Theatre Festival at the Gaiety in 1961. She had no real feeling for Brecht's epic theatre; nor had the director, Hilton Edwards, despite his technical mastery, any deep understanding of the required '"alienation" effect. He seems to have given Siobhán her head in the choice of the American actor William Marshall for the male lead. Set in the Chicago meat-packing jungle of 1930, after the Great Depression, Brecht's piece had little – apart from vague aspirations to martyrdom – in common with the real Joan of Arc. The evangelist of the title, like Shaw's Major Barbara, tried to feed Chicago's hungry unemployed with soup and socialist hymns. Unaccustomed to the Marxian dialectic which ordained that capitalism can only be overthrown by revolt, Saint Joan of the Stockyards dies because she recoils from the use of violence. It held little appeal for the Dublin audiences and even less for Siobhán before its short run ended. In the angry scene where Joan Dark, as she is called, drives the modern money-changers from the temple, she looked like Little Bo-Peep driving sheep to the fair. Despite the failure, a few years later Siobhán took over from Vanessa Redgrave, when she had to withdraw from a London production, directed by Tony Richardson at the Queen's Theatre, London, in 1964. Lacking Vanessa Redgrave's strong leftist convictions, Siobhán's Marxist "voices" failed her once more. One would have liked to have seen her in a much superior Brecht play *Mother Courage,* with a director who would not allow her to play the traditional heroic mother who gives her all for her children, rather than the scheming survivor of the Thirty Years War that the author intended.

On New Year's Eve 1961, Siobhán was in at the start of Irish television in a bilingual recital with MacLiammóir in which she proclaimed:

Mise Éire,
Sinne mé ná an Cailleach Béara.
Mór mo ghlóir
Mé do rug Cuchulainn Cróga.[27]

I am Ireland,
Older than the Hag of Beara.
Great is my glory
I that bore Cuchulainn the Brave.

But the great new viewing audience seemed more interested in the spectacle of Ireland's entertainers being snow-balled by gurriers in O'Connell Street than in excursions into the mythic past. The swinging sixties had arrived in Dublin to find Siobhán still marching to a different beat. Never a whiner, if she could not help herself to get better parts, she would do her best for others. After an unrewarding and unremarkable performance as Lady Cicely in *Captain Brassbound's Conversion* at the Gaiety, she volunteered to direct the first professional production of *Daughter From Over the Water* by the Galway playwright M.J. Molloy, whom she regarded as "the most exquisite stylist in the theatre since Synge". His earlier plays, *The King of Friday's Men*, *The Wood of the Whispering* and *The Paddy Pedlar* were elegiac evocations of a vanishing Ireland. He had tried in *Daughter From Over the Water* to handle a more contemporary rural problem with a light-hearted farcical approach. When the play was rejected by the Abbey, who had staged most of his work, he was naturally dejected and felt out-of-touch with the professional theatre. His only consolation was that the play proved popular on the amateur circuit. Long an admirer of Molloy's work, Siobhán had made the journey to Castlerea, Co. Roscommon, for the first amateur production of *Daughter From Over the Water*. She liked what she saw and promised on the spot to try to find the time and money to give the play a professional production.

The piece was a curious hybrid, part farce, part "religious problem play", indigestible fare for a Dublin audience in 1964. The farcical bit concerned a ne'er-do-well farmer who spends his time composing lugubrious laments for *Old Moore's Almanac*, while his cattle stray into his neighbours' fields. Only the impending marriage of his daughter "over the water" in a London registry office, to a professed atheist, arouses the so-called farmer from his versifying. In order to save his daughter from "a fate worse than death", the father pretends to be dead himself to hasten her return for his funeral. When she does arrive, with the connivance of the family and neighbours, she is a witness to the supposed miraculous resurrection of her father.

As well as trying to direct this bucolic morality play, Siobhán cast herself as a scarecrow of a spinster "on the verge of matrimony". After the daughter is reunited with Mother Church and her husband-to-be, the farmer's fortunes are restored, and as in all the best pantomimes, no fewer than three happy couples are lined up for the final curtain so that the audience can rest assured that "they all lived happily ever after".

Fake miracles are about as theatrically effective as moving statues, but perhaps out of deference to Molloy and Siobhán most of the critics were more than kind. She may have turned her spinster part into "a little gem of farcical comedy", but the whole expensive undertaking raised serious questions about Siobhán's prospects as an actor/manager.

She showed better judgement when she urged the Abbey to stage Heno Magee's *Hatchet*. The story goes that Heno's father arrived one day at Siobhán's house to cut hedges. Knowing that she was a famous actress, he was not slow to let her know that his son had written a play he "wanted her to read". She recognised the merits of the piece as a rather terrifying exposé of the violence and gang warfare which was endemic in the inner city. First produced at the Peacock Theatre in 1972, it was successfully revived under Joe Dowling's direction on the bigger Abbey stage a few years later. Siobhán neither sought nor received any credit.

Siobhán's appearances in London had been infrequent since her stage triumph as Pegeen Mike. If she did not always succeed in getting the parts she wanted, she made her own of the parts that came her way. She was fortunate that after a try-out run at Brighton, she startled the London critics in a play they did not greatly like, Jean Anouilh's *The Cavern,* at the Strand Theatre. Again she was cast as an earth-mother character, Marie Jeanne, once the concubine of the Lord of the Manor but now a prisoner of her own past. She meets a sticky end as a drudge of a cook in the kitchen downstairs. There is as much of Pirandello as of Anouilh in this puzzling theatrical *mélange*. Instead of six characters in search of an author, one has the author on stage in search of his characters and the murderer. A clever spoof of the complex plot was written by the *Sunday Telegraph* critic, Alan Brien, as if Maigret himself were on the case:

> "Well, *patron*, as far as I can establish the facts, it looks as though the murdered cook had once been mistress of her employer, the Count, though for the last twenty years she has been living with the Count's Coachman. She had also quite a local reputation for cooking up potions which helped abort young

servant girls pregnant (though she did not know this) by her lover.

"Her last patient, the kitchen-maid, was in love with the cook's illegitimate son by the Count, a young seminarist, but she is now in a brothel in Algiers picked out for her by the Valet who runs a white-slave trading post in his spare time."

"*Merci*, Lucas. A typically *banal*, and run-of-the-moulin crime for such a fashionable *quartier* of Paris. Any of the boys working on it?"

"Yes, I mean *bien sûr, patron*. Two Inspectors who have found out not too much and now a Superintendent who is determined to find out nothing. The Count is a *bon ami* of the Prefect. Shall we go there?"

"No, Lucas, my authority is no longer recognised at the Strand Theatre. But I can assure you that *la règle de jeu* ensures that none of the obvious subjects will be guilty. Is there not perhaps drifting around a suspicious character with a shaggy moustache and steel-rimmed spectacles who answers to the alias of Author?"

"*Patron,* you are formidable. There is indeed. He said everything that has happened comes from a play he didn't write. But how come could you know he was here?"

"I read about him in the critics' reviews, my old one. A good detective can find information anywhere – even in a newspaper."[28]

One can only speculate what Flann O'Brien, alias Myles na Gopaleen, would have made of it, but Siobhán left the critics in no doubt about what she could do with such unpromising material:

Miss McKenna is never less than magnificent. Here, with her wild Titian hair like some unquenchable flame, was a woman who faced life full square. Her eyes held that unblinkered bravery, that unflinching defiance, which deals as brutally with life as life deserves.

Her voice rang with an authoritative acceptance which held one in utter awe.

She had only to murmur flatly, "Yes, my Tom-Tit, I have a score to settle with love," for one to know exactly what a contemptuously fragile thing she had found life to be. She said it with the bitter wisdom born of centuries of suffering ... But my tears were all for the tough Marie Jeanne as she lay dying, clutching the dented gilt crown she had once worn when she was a carnival queen for a day.

Of course, such a queen among women deserved a crown. But perhaps the fact that she had kept it by her showed that even she needed one small illusion to make life and death less painful, that and the comfort of one fellow creature [the Author] who cared.[29]

Brigid Chapman drew attention to Siobhán's unquestionable magnetism when she was given or gave herself half a chance:

Irish actress Siobhán McKenna has that rare quality of repose that gives such depth to every scene in which she is involved. She can stand motionless, a shaft of light focused on her face, and give pathos and point to the interplay of characters in another part of the composite set.

When she rages she is a matriarch to be feared and when she mothers she is protective but not possessive. Always she has dignity even unto death.[30]

There were parallels between Siobhán's achievement and the upstairs downstairs, topsy turveydom of *The Cavern*. Such virtuosity was regarded by some critics as little more than the conjuror's trick of telling the audience that he is going to let them into the secret of how it is actually done, only to baffle them further by an admission that he has forgotten how he did it in the first place. The well-made boulevard play of Anouilh's day and its English equivalent as written by Terence Rattigan or Noel Coward were swept aside by the social realism and the zany rhythms of the sixties. Actors like McKenna and MacLiammóir looked and sounded out of fashion. Television reduced everything to a banal naturalism ill-suited to the great classical parts. Siobhán could never be counted among those players Yeats excoriated:

But actors lacking music
Do most excite my spleen,
They say it is more human
To shuffle, grunt and groan,
Not knowing what unearthly stuff
Rounds a mighty scene.[31]

The lines of Shakespeare and Synge were chopped and mangled into a mish-mash which was supposed to appeal to a mass public who never went to the theatre in the first place. As one Shakespearean actor put it, "It was not good theatre if you could deliver 'To be or not to be' without coughing or blowing your nose."[32]

Siobhán felt she was now ready for the poetic realism of the great O'Casey roles. When Fred O'Donovan of Eamon Andrews Productions lined up Peter O'Toole as Captain Boyle and Jack MacGowran as Joxer, she jumped at the chance to play Juno at the Gaiety Theatre, Dublin, in 1966. All three actors were new to the roles and the director, Denis Carey, would be the first to admit that his experience in O'Casey was limited. This three-star *Juno and the Paycock* was a sure-fire box-office attraction, but no sooner did rehearsals begin than there were temperamental clashes and rows. As Jack MacGowran was filming by day in London for Roman Polanski in *Dance of the Vampires*, the first rehearsals were held there in the evening. Siobhán was unnerved by what she saw at rehearsals. "As I arrived, Denis Carey and the co-producer Jules Buck had Jackie pinned against the wall. 'You do one or the other – the play or the film,' they told him."[33] McGowran did both at great risk to his health. The rehearsal schedule greatly annoyed O'Toole, who regarded stage work as a slight diversion from the more serious business of making a great amount of money in movies. He was a bit of a firebrand in those days and thought of MacGowran as a puppet on a string. Five years earlier during a Shakespearean season at Stratford on Avon, they had shared many binges and hangovers in the Dirty Duck. MacGowran was on the verge of a breakdown from the double rehearsal stint and partying late at night with Polanski. Much to O'Toole's disgust, MacGowran actually collapsed and rehearsals were cancelled until he recovered. He had come to resemble one of those despairing Beckett characters which he played so strikingly. "Jackie became so engrossed in Beckett, you couldn't draw him out of himself," explained Siobhán. "But then you'd mention something and his face would light up as if you had reminded him of the person he'd been before he became so completely absorbed in his work."[34]

O'Toole's Captain Boyle was all swagger and dramatic pauses. As someone said of another film star, he had his *simple* pause, his *middle* pause, and his *grand* pause, while the rhythm of O'Casey's speech was drowned in a staccato Liverpudlian accent which surprised many who believed him when he said he was born in Connemara. He was cleverly upstaged by the more muted MacGowran who gave Dublin audiences a Joxer the likes of which they had never seen.

"This Joxer," wrote Seamus Kelly in *The Irish Times*, "is a cross between a Shakespearean fool and a gutter rat, packed with jerkily visual comedy but basically full of the sort of rodent malignancy that bares its teeth when the people it sponges on meet disaster. It's a terrifying, powerful performance, one that will be remembered with respect – and a lot of unease."[35]

Siobhán's Juno, "based on a Dublin woman who worked as a cleaner in the Gaiety", was clearly in the Abbey mode – a near flawless performance that only fell short of greatness by an occasional slide into a Connemara cadence. In this respect, she lacked the superb confidence of Eileen Crowe. The overall production lacked cohesion in that the three principals, Juno, Captain Boyle and Joxer, never seemed to be acting in the same play. There was action and acting in plenty, but no reaction or reacting. The great verbal skirmishes between Joxer and the Captain and between Juno and her Paycock sounded more like set pieces by solo performers. This approach was proper for May Craig who each night as Mrs Tancred, with her wonderful solo speech, virtually brought the play to a halt. Siobhán loved to tell the story of how her old friend May used to do her Mrs Tancred at parties, and occasionally at the top of Grafton Street when egged on by brats of actors who said that they never tired of listening to her.

O'Toole was up to some outrageous tricks on stage. He tried to make Siobhán giggle when he had his back to the audience by putting cigarettes up his nostrils. But she certainly did not giggle when answering an off-stage call from the Captain to bring the *News of the World* to his bedroom; she went to the door with the paper only to see O'Toole in the wings peeing into a stout bottle. She threatened "to have him up for indecent exposure" if he ever tried it again. This prankster was one of those invited to her great after-show parties which sometimes went on all night at Highfield Road. Donnacha recalled that he woke up one Sunday morning to go to mass and saw through his window O'Toole trying to jump into the goldfish pond. Now in his late teens, he enjoyed the fun but became bored with the endless chatter about the theatre. The worst offenders were the uninvited latecomers who invariably wanted to stay until morning.

Unlike the offspring of most professionals, Donnacha never had a great interest in the stage and even succeeded in avoiding school plays at Synge Street by making known his determination to be a champion swimmer. Of course, he went to see her play, but he always thought of Siobhán as a loving mother who happened to spend a lot of time away from home and showered him with gifts on her return, rather than as a great actress. He liked her particularly in *Laurette*, staged for the Dublin Theatre Festival in 1964, in which she played the part of the alcoholic actress, Laurette Taylor, once the Broadway star of *Peg O' My Heart* and *The Glass Menagerie*. It was a nerve-wracking week for Siobhán, during which she lost her voice but continued to play, only to have *The Irish Times* dismiss the piece as "alien corn".

Swimming meant a great deal to Donnacha; it was his way of escaping from the make-believe and tinsel of stage life. Although Siobhán was part of that world she liked to claim that she kept in touch with a more mundane reality by going with Donnacha to visit her sister. Nancy had married an architect, Patrick McMahon, and lived in a nice house with land and cattle in the foothills of the Dublin mountains. At school the other pupils thought that because both of his parents were actors Donnacha was the only child of rich parents. But he knew the insecurity of an actor's life, earning and spending hundreds per week for three or four months and then "resting", waiting for something to turn up for the remainder of the year. Siobhán worried when, after a term doing business studies at Trinity College, he went one better than his father by becoming a bookmaker and a professional poker player of international class. He has since made several trips to Las Vegas where he has played successfully against some of the greatest of the high rollers.

Donnacha had been swimming since the age of three but did not swim competitively until he was thirteen. When they went swimming together at Williamstown, Denis liked Donnacha to train seriously by doing a good sprint or two before lolling about on the beach. Although facilities for training were woefully inadequate, he was Irish champion for the hundred metres for several years and was chosen to represent Ireland at the Mexico Olympics in 1968.

"It meant that my mother's name did not cast a shadow over me anymore," he half jocosely told a journalist. "I made a name for myself in my own field. ... It made me a lot more independent, too. My mother jokes now that she is known as the swimmer's mother. First she was Professor Eoin McKenna's daughter. Then he was Siobhán McKenna's father. Now she is Donnacha O'Dea's mother."[36]

Professor Eoin McKenna died on 29 January 1967, and, as he wished, his coffin was carried to the grave in Rahoon on the shoulders of the great Galway footballers of the fifties and sixties, many of whom had known him as one of their greatest supporters in the Sigerson Cup and All-Ireland championships. He had carried his knowledge of mathematics lightly. As Siobhán had said, he saw poetry in a problem in calculus. He wanted his students, including Siobhán, to share his enjoyment. "The students liked him," said Siobhán, "because he helped them to pass their examinations. He insisted that the teacher's job was to find out how much his students knew, not how much they didn't know."[37]

Prior to the opening of the new Abbey Theatre in 1966, the government appointed Denis O'Dea as one of the twenty-five new shareholders who were to aid and advise the Abbey directors in the formation of the theatre's policy. Apart from the inaugural meeting in Government Buildings in 1965, Denis never attended a meeting. Although in earlier years he had been treasurer of the Writers, Artists, Actors and Musicians Association (later Irish Actors Equity), he was never a committee man. In the mid-sixties, he gave up his acting career, never returned to the new Abbey as guest artist, and spent most of his time with his poker-playing pals, Teddy Rice and Cedric Callaghan. He had an occasional "touch" at the races, especially when he had information from the Rogers stable who turned out Hard Ridden and Santa Claus to win Epsom derbies.

Siobhán had been nominated with Denis as one of ten life-members of the Abbey Theatre company who, according to the citation, "had given distinguished service to the Irish National Theatre" and who had agreed to play as guest artists with the regular company from time to time. T.P. McKenna is the only survivor as Siobhán and Denis, Jack MacGowran, Ria Mooney, Micheál MacLiammóir, Ray MacAnally, Shelah Richards, Arthur Shields and Cyril Cusack have all sadly made their last exits.

Each of the ten life members was presented with a parchment scroll with Yeats's tribute to the Abbey players:

> We playwrights can only thank those players who have given us the delight of seeing our work so well performed, working with so much enthusiasm, and with so much patience, that they have found for themselves a lasting place among the artists, the only aristocracy that has never been sold in the market or seen the people rise up against it.[38]

This well-intentioned and richly deserved tribute to the recipients of the scroll aroused petty jealousy among some who thought they should have been included. There was an effort to have certain names removed. As a result, no further names were added to the original list. The first players to honour the commitment to appear as guest artists at what was then the top salary for a senior Abbey actor (£26 per week) were Cyril Cusack as Conn in *The Shaughraun* and Siobhán as Cass in *The Loves of Cass Maguire*. The part had been written by Brian Friel with Siobhán in mind. The role was not made for her, as has been said; she made it for herself. She played it on BBC radio, but when the play was first staged on Broadway it flopped, Ruth Gordon being badly miscast in the part. This was a shattering blow to Brian Friel and the director Hilton Edwards. Brendan Smith had plans for an Olympia production, but Siobhán accepted Tomás MacAnna's invitation to play under his direction at the Abbey, although she would have had a much higher salary at the Olympia.

The Cass of the title is a blowzy, boozy, vulgar Irish-American emigrant who, after a lifetime working in menial jobs, returns from the States to a home that is no longer there. She has slaved all her life to send home a few dollars to her family, who do not want her money, having made good in the bourgeois Ireland of the post-war period. Not only do they not want her dollars, they do not want her either. She is a walking caricature of what they might have been if they hadn't done well for themselves. Her randy laughter, her floppy flowery dresses, her blue-rinsed wig, her cheap costume jewellery would have made her the laughing stock of her native town, if her relatives had not persuaded her to become an inmate of the ironically named Eden Home, where she can salvage something of her lost loves and shattered illusions. Much of Brian Friel's best writing approximates to music and Siobhán was perfectly attuned to the melodic flow between the past and the present, between the daydream and the reality. The play is a concerto with Siobhán as a magnificent soloist. Like the other inmates of Eden Home, she at last gets a kind of release as she sits in the winged chair of fantasy, in which she can escape from a brood she believed to be dependent on her.

As an earth-mother of the sleazy New York sidewalks, Siobhán played with a gusto and extravagance that was heightened by Tomás MacAnna's sensitive and unobtrusive direction. Friel, who does not hold the directorial control of modern theatre in high regard, told MacAnna that at last he had seen the play as he had written it. It may not rank as his greatest play, but Friel had created a great role for a real star. Siobhán did not shirk looking awful for a change. Her costume and make-up were as outrageous as her splutters and spits. She wore wads of padding all over. An American matron who had seen her as Saint Joan could not believe her eyes. "My God," she exclaimed. "How she has deteriorated!" It was at Siobhán's suggestion that Cass makes her last exit high as a coot singing "I'm a Yankee Doodle Dandy", a change which Friel included in the published text.

During the rehearsals of *The Loves of Cass Maguire*, Siobhán first met Niall Buggy, a handsome nineteen-year-old actor who immediately fell under her spell:

> "I'm Siobhán. What's your name?"
> "Buggy. Niall Buggy."
> "Buggy," she roared laughing. "What a funny name!"
> She told him he was "something special" and wanted him to stay in the Abbey to perfect his craft. "She was genuinely committed to the notion of the Abbey. The Abbey had a special quality because of the company."[39]

Knowing that Denis O'Dea was a non-attender at shareholders' meetings, I asked Siobhán one day if she would allow me, as chairman of the Abbey Board, to nominate her for election as a shareholder. She agreed to this but added somewhat coyly, "If I'm elected, I'll be asking the Abbey to give good parts to Niall Buggy." Taken aback, I do not recall exactly what I said in reply, probably that it would be no concern of the shareholders. Siobhán was a free spirit, expecting in her personal life as much freedom as her male peers.

When *The Cherry Orchard* is mentioned, comparisons are sometimes made between Chekov's Russia and the plight of Ireland's landed gentry in the nineteenth century. I recall the night of an Abbey party when Siobhán and Cyril Cusack spent a happy hour drawing parallels between *The Lament for Kilcash* and *The Cherry Orchard*.

> *Cad a dhéanfaimíd feasta gan adhmad*
> *Tá deireadh na gcoillte ar lár;*
> *Níl trácht ar Chill Chais ná a theaghlach*
> *Is ní cluinfear a cling go bráth.*

What shall we do now for timber
With the last of the woods laid low;
There's no talk of Cill Cais or its people
Its great bell will ring no more.

It was fanciful, perhaps, to compare the bountiful Lady Butler of
Kilcash with the capricious, flighty Madame Ranevskaya, who
owned not only the cherry orchard but thousands of serfs. But there
had been a recent production of a BBC radio play, *The Light of
Other Days*, in which Chekov's play had been adapted to an Irish
setting. It was not a particularly novel idea. As Cyril pointed out,
Lennox Robinson had been doing this for over twenty years in plays
like *Killycreggs at Twilight*. The conversation drifted to parallels
between the Moscow Art Theatre and the Abbey, particularly the
interesting coincidence that in the same year as Yeats, Lady Gregory
and Edward Martyn met to launch the Irish Literary Theatre in
opposition to the commercial theatre of the 1890s, two young
Russians, Stanislavsky and Nemirovich-Danchenko, dissatisfied
with the Czarist theatre, resolved to found the new and revolutionary Moscow Art Theatre. Their first production was in a barn,
some thirty miles from Moscow, on an improvised stage. Likewise,
the Irish experiment had to overcome the inadequate facilities of the
Antient Concert Rooms and the limitations of English actors as
speakers of Yeats's verse until the brothers Willie and Frank Fay
formed a company of Irish actors who subsequently became known
as the first Abbey Theatre company. In order to forge another link in
the chain of thought, Cyril and Siobhán thought it would be a
splendid idea to invite a Moscow Art Theatre director who had
worked with Stanislavsky to come to the Abbey for a production of
The Cherry Orchard. Siobhán declared an interest in the part of
Madame Ranevskaya and teasingly began to play verbal Russian
roulette, trying to find out from Cyril what part he would like to
play. Impishly, she suggested that he would be great as Firs, the old
retainer who had little or nothing to say but is left alone on stage to
die at the final curtain. Cyril hummed but didn't haw, saying he
would leave the casting to the Moscow Arts director. Later he
roguishly told Tomás MacAnna, the Abbey's artistic director, that he
would like to play Trominov, the young student.
    The Dublin Theatre Festival paid the expenses of the visiting
director, Madame Maria Knebel, who had been selected by the

Cultural Division of the Russian Embassy in London, as Ireland had no diplomatic link with Soviet Russia in those years. A small, lively woman with Slavic features, Madame Knebel had studied under Stanislavsky and had played many character parts with the Moscow Art Theatre, including Charlotta in *The Cherry Orchard*. She had more English than she pretended, but only spoke through an interpreter from the Russian department of Trinity College. Tomás MacAnna had lined up a tentative cast for her approval and Cyril Cusack ended up with the part of Gayev, which, no doubt, he had intended to play anyhow. Siobhán also had her way with Madame Ranevskaya and was even more delighted with the casting of Niall Buggy as Trominov.

True to the poetic profundity of Chekov, Madame Knebel emphasised the universality of the play. "Every one of us has lost our own cherry orchard," she explained. "We try to hold on to it but when it is lost, it seems that everything is lost. ... But our whole life is before us, the life that is a thousand times richer than our losses. And the sense of life is the life-giving force that gives us the courage to live."[40]

She was disappointed when she learned that she had only four weeks to rehearse, as against the four months she would have had in Moscow. For the decor, she draped the high Abbey stage in transparent white tulle against an off-white backcloth. The furnishings, even the piano and the sideboard, were covered in cream covers. For the ballroom scene, a crystal chandelier was dropped from the flies. A dozen bare trees indicated a roadside. The only colour came from the bright costumes of the period, 1904. One never saw the mystical cherry orchard, which remained in the mind of the audience, except for a rose tint cast at times on the white drapes. Unlike the neo-naturalism and over-elaboration of set design which had become the norm, as the theatre foolishly tried to compete with the meticulous realism of cinema and television, this austere, spare and imaginative staging in no way diminished the actors but allowed them a freedom of movement which sustained the rhythmic flow of the piece.

According to Madame Knebel, the Abbey cast lived up to their reputation of being different:

The first rehearsal was not the best of introductions. The actors were late, they rambled unhurriedly into the rehearsal room chatting animatedly with glasses of whiskey or cups of coffee in their hands. Some of them proceeded to sit down – on the floor!

110

This sort of approach could only portend disaster. "What on earth are we going to accomplish in a month?" I thought.

I cannot remember exactly what I said on this first occasion. Probably something banal like the small amount of time we had and the precious value of each minute of it. It wasn't what I said but the obvious emotion in my voice, which triggered off a response in these artists' hearts.

"Madame, there will be no repetition of this," said Cyril Cusack, who was to play the part of Gayev. He talked for a while with the others and his words were met with nods and sounds of approval. Without further ado, a decision was made for that month to waive trade union rules and privileges gained by long and arduous negotiation and strife. It was decided that the work would go on with a break of only one hour. So they decided; so they promised me, and I am proud to say that not once in the course of that month did anyone break their word. Most evenings some of my "Abbey" actors were involved in the current Abbey play, but the others continued rehearsals up to a late hour ... They simply did not accept the notion of technique rehearsals, but gave of their best at even the most casual run-through. Every rehearsal was for them a performance. This was typical of the "Yeats School" of technical mastery![41]

Whatever about the "Yeats School", which she said resembled the Stanislavsky School, Madame Knebel had the happy knack of getting the Abbey actors to work much harder than they would for one of their own. Siobhán's only complaint was that Cyril Cusack sucked sweets during some of her best lines.

Theories about "images" and "presentation" simply disgusted them. I remember Siobhán McKenna, who played Madame Ranevskaya, laughing heartily at one of the players who was adding "bits of business" to his part. "Nobody will accept that," she remarked, and I think that simple comment had more influence than a whole dissertation on theatrical truth.[42]

Siobhán and Cyril did not overshadow the rest of the cast and the production was hailed as "a landmark in the Irish theatre":

As the dispossessed owner, [Siobhán McKenna] gives the best performance of her career. Gorgeous in sweeping velvet and black plumes, she catches every mood of the generous, attractive and temperamental woman who has thrown her life away in frivolities. Cyril Cusack is equally magnificent in his portrayal of the charming ineffectual Gayev. The third key figure is Lopakhin, the speculator, and Geoffrey Golden matches the two virtuosos with a performance of real power and sympathy torn between a genuine desire to help the family and his own self interest. One admired all the other performances enormously ...[43]

The *Sunday Times* critic J. W. Lambert wrote:

... but of all the Gayevs I have seen, perhaps, I shall remember Cyril Cusack's the best; he married his own brand of hesitation perfectly to the ageing fusspot's garrulity. And Siobhán McKenna's restrained Madame Ranevskaya was entirely a woman whose physical prime hardly concealed her spiritual collapse. Her stillness, and the slow turn of her head towards her brother, as they stood for the last time in the old house, caught the emotion hanging in the air like a shot bird in the moment before it tumbles to earth.[44]

One must search diligently for a dissenting voice. There is one in every audience. Peter Roberts, in *Plays and Players,* said that Siobhán was "more pert chambermaid than venerable chatelaine".[45] Madame Knebel's final memory was one of laughter:

Ranevskaya and Gayev became real living characters, all the more so for the Irish people since they weren't "businessmen". The attitudes of this impractical pair evoked much sympathetic and kindly laughter from the cast at rehearsals, and later from the audiences. Ranevskaya's line, "We must have a party" unfailingly got a laugh. "She hasn't any money," they would say to me, "and yet she wants to throw a party. Marvelous!"[46]

Siobhán hadn't any money but she continued "to throw a party". Like Cyril Cusack, she had made some sacrifice to help the Abbey by playing for a meagre salary of twenty-six pounds a week. In Siobhán's case, the loss was the harder to bear as neither of her indelibly memorable performances in *The Loves of Cass Maguire* or in *The Cherry Orchard* were seen in London or in America.

The roaring girl of earlier years had mellowed, but she still needed the panoply of success: her designer Irish tweeds, her Norwegian elk-hound, Rory, and a fun fur coat. When she was miscast in

London productions like *Play with a Tiger* (1962), *On a Foggy Day* (1969) and *Best of Friends* (1970), she over-compensated by drawing attention to herself, showing up the shoddiness of the parts. In quiet desperation at the lack of new opportunities, she decided to do something completely different for a change.

Notes

1. Letter from Mary Frances McHugh to Siobhán McKenna, 6 December 1953
2. Harold Hobson, *Sunday Times*, 16 October 1960
3. *Punch*, 19 October 1960
4. Harold Hobson, op. cit.
5. *Daily Telegraph,* interview with Siobhán McKenna, 25 July 1970
6. Bernard Levin, *Daily Express*, 13 October 1960
7. Ibid.
8. Ulick O'Connor, *Brendan Behan: A Biography* (Hamish Hamilton, 1970) p.183
9. Kenneth Tynan, *Observer*, 16 October 1960
10. *Tribune*, 21 October 1960
11. Eric Johns, interview with Siobhán McKenna, *The Stage*, 20 October 1960
12. Ibid.
13. Máire Nic Shuibhlaigh, edited by Edward Kenny Duffy, *The Splendid Years* (1955) p.42
14. Thomas Wiseman, interview with Siobhán McKenna, *Evening Standard*, 14 October 1960
15. Ken Massingham, interview with Siobhán McKenna, *Sunday Dispatch,* 16 October 1960
16. *The Kerryman*, 8 July 1961 and 8 August, 1961
17. Interview with Mrs Bridie Foley, Inch, 9 April 1991
18. Interview with Donnacha O'Dea, 10 March 1992
19. Sheila Walsh, interview with Siobhán McKenna, *Irish Press*, 19 August 1961
20. *Films in Review: An Annual 1962*, pp.368-69
21. *Newsweek*, 31 December 1962
22. Lady Gregory, *Our Irish Theatre*, (G.B. Putman, 1913) p.229
23. Ibid.
24. F.C.P., *Waterbury Republican*, 18 December 1967
25. Don Rubin, *New Haven Register*, 17 December 1967
26. *Irish Press*, 21 June 1977
27. P.H. Pearse, *The 1916 Poets* (Talbot Press)

28. *Sunday Telegraph*, 14 November 1965
29. *Evening Argus*, 12 October 1965
30. *Brighton and Howe Review*, 15 October 1965
31. W.B. Yeats, "The Old Stone Cross," *Last Poems* (Macmillan, 1960)
32. John Nettle of the RSC, *Irish Times*, 1 October 1983
33. Jordan R. Young, *The Beckett Actor* (The Moonstone Press, 1987) p.152
34. Ibid.
35. *Irish Times*, 3 August 1966
36. *Evening Post*, 15 February 1968
37. Padraic Ó Raghallaigh, interview with Siobhán McKenna, RTE 1983
38. W. B. Yeats, *Samhain*, 1904
39. Interview with Niall Buggy, March 1993
40. Programme note for *The Cherry Orchard*, 1969
41. Madame Knebel, *Sovietskaya Kultura*, translated for *Irish Times*, 28 January 1969
42. Ibid.
43. Maureen O'Farrell, *Evening Press*, 13 October 1968
44. J.W. Lambert, *Sunday Times*, 13 October 1968
45. *Plays and Players*, December 1968, p.65
46. Madame Knebel, *Sovietskaya Kultura*, *Irish Times*, 28 January 1969

Solo Flights

IN THE FIFTIES I ran a radio series, *My Kind of Poetry*, in which people from diverse backgrounds read their favourite "pieces", with a few introductory remarks on the reasons for their choice. It might have been more appropriately called "My Kind of Recitation" because it embraced nearly everything from "The Croppy Boy" to "The Green Eye of the Little Yellow God". Whenever she was free, Siobhán never refused to come along to the old radio studios on the roof of the General Post Office to record her favourite verse. She was nearly always late for the inadequate rehearsal and arrived breathless with lame excuses about taxis that had broken down or road repairs in Rathgar. She usually had a handbag full of various anthologies of Irish poetry. The selection of material was a haphazard affair and she spent a great deal of time rifling through the pages in search of this poem or that. As her choices were fairly predictable, it struck me that this was a mere ploy to get her breath back before the start of the recording; even after starting she would ad-lib nonchalantly while searching for the right page. If she were really stuck, she would launch into Maurya's great lament from *Riders to the Sea*, which she knew by heart: "They are all gone now and there isn't anything more the sea can do to me ..." and so on to: "No man at all can be living forever and we must be satisfied." In the meantime she would have found "The Mother" by Pearse, which she invariably included. It was difficult to get her not to recite it.

115

Most people who worked with her found it hard to be critical of Siobhán. She was a star who never acted the part of the diva or prima donna. If one proffered an opinion she did not like, she would not contradict but look a little sadly past you into the middle distance as if she had not heard. Beneath the confusion and above the clouds of cigarette smoke and the auburn tresses she was always brushing from her face, there was an inner calm and composure which was reassuring. Once she got over the jitters, she could woo the microphone like a bee at a honeysuckle. As you listened to those honeyed tones, you really believed that she was not performing for the money but to help you or somebody else out of a tight corner. Thanks or compliments were returned with a friendly smile.

She was more organised when invited to appear at charity concerts. There were few Sundays – the actors' free day – when she did not appear at gala concerts, "midnight matinées" or fund-raising shows, often on a no-fee basis. In an evening gown and the minimum of make-up, she usually included a speech from Saint Joan or Synge and a selection from Yeats's anthology pieces. She had to play to the gallery with a crowd who had come to hear Jimmy O'Dea or Maureen Potter. These charity shows were usually followed by late night parties either on stage or in hotel ballrooms. Even off-stage, she usually looked the tallest woman as she moved across a crowded room. She was practically a chain smoker and had a drink with every group she joined, even if it was only for a few minutes. She had a great head for spirits, which seemed to have little effect on her except that she laughed more heartily than usual. In the theatre, the cast always knew when Siobhán was in the audience, as she laughed encouragingly at every opportunity. There were other actors who sat like tombstones, especially on a first night. A well-known comedian once described a first-night Dublin audience as "A Pilgrimage to Knock". When Siobhán herself was on stage, she did not want to know if there were celebrities attending, as she liked to play to an audience as a single entity rather than to a mixum-gatherum of conflicting egos.

For over a decade, Siobhán had vague ideas of compiling a one-woman show. The one-woman show was a rarity in these islands in the sixties, although Ruth Draper and Cornelia Otis Skinner had long before made their own of the genre on the other side of the Atlantic. Siobhán said that Micheál MacLiammóir had suggested the idea to her. It was to be planned on the lines of his *I Must Be*

Talking to My Friends, but Siobhán was so uncertain about how to tackle it that she said she was going to call it I Must Be Talking to Myself. She dreaded the task of writing a linking script for the excerpts from the poetry, novels and plays that she had used for radio, television and gala concerts over the years.

At an after-theatre party at the Beckett Theatre, founded by Francis Warner in Oxford, Siobhán was persuaded to do bits and pieces from plays in which she had appeared. Wolf Mankowitz and Laurence Harvey, who were present, insisted that she should quit her happy-go-lucky approach and get down to serious work. More importantly, they were prepared as successful men of the theatre to put up the money with a view to a West End opening.

She borrowed her title, *Here Are Ladies*, from James Stephens's collection of stories, poems and sketches, and returned the compliment by opening her show with his subtle and quirky poem, "A Woman is a Branchy Tree":

A woman is a branchy tree
And man a singing wind

And from her branches carelessly
He takes what he can find.

The wind and man go far away
While winter comes with loneliness
With cold and rain, and slow decay
On woman and on tree, till they

Droop to the earth again, and be
A withered woman, a withered tree;
While wind and man woo in the glade
Another tree, another maid.[1]

This was far from a clarion call for feminism and Siobhán's haunting voice sounded like that "singing wind" about to possess her. She whimsically introduced Stephens as Ireland's greatest leprechaun poet and as the satirical humorist who wrote her next piece, that wonderful dialogue between the thin woman and the fat woman of Inismagrath from *The Crock of Gold*.

She was determined that nothing stage-Irish or schmaltzy would be included, like the verses she was frequently urged to recite by the American Irish:

T'anam chun Dia, but there it is –
The dawn on the hills of Ireland!
God's angels lifting the night's black veil
From the fair, sweet face of my sireland!

O Ireland! isn't it grand you look –
Like a bride in her rich adornin'!
With all the pent-up love of my heart
I bid you the top o' the mornin'.[2]

A try-out production was planned for the Oxford Playhouse, where it was suggested that she should be billed as a *diseuse*, but when she heard a Dublin impresario pronounce this as a "disease", she wisely decided to take no risks. She had now enlisted her good friend Seán Kenny to act as her designer/director. He had first made news as an architectural student who had sailed the Atlantic in the yacht *Ituna* to pursue his studies under Frank Lloyd Wright. Later he became famous as the designer of the sets for the musical *Oliver* and for Brendan Behan's *The Hostage*. His choice of three tall standing stones or monoliths bathed in a green light, with incidental music predictably by Seán Ó Riada, captured an heroic mood even if it reminded the less imaginative of Stonehenge.

The inclusion of some unlady-like interludes required that a rack of hats, scarves and shawls had to be provided outside of the magic ring. There was such a variety of headgear required that one caustic reviewer suggested an alternative title, "Here Are Hats". It certainly fitted her opening scene from *The Plough and the Stars*, where Ginnie Gogan peeps into the parcel that has come from Arnotts for her fashion-conscious tenement neighbour Nora Clitheroe:

"I wonder what's this now? A hat! God, she's going to the devil lately for style. That hat now cost more than a penny. Such notions of upperosity she's gettin'! Oh swank, what!"

This leads naturally into her dissertation with Mr Fluther Good in which she shows "a trespassin' joy" in her account of deaths, hearses and funerals. In turn this is the cue for a switch to a more tragic moment with Mrs Tancred's famous lament in *Juno and the Paycock* for her dead son:

"Sacred Heart of the crucified Jesus, take away our hearts of stone ... and give us hearts of flesh ... Take away this murderin' hate ... and give us thine own eternal love!"

She retreats into the shadows and emerges with a shawl slung around her shoulders to become Maurya, the heartbroken old mother of *Riders to the Sea*, intoning for the umpteenth time:

"They're all gone now and there isn't anything more the sea can do to me ..."

Her great speech to her judges from *Saint Joan* is lightly introduced by one of her favourite anecdotes. Shaw, she said, sent two tickets to Churchill for the first night of *Saint Joan* with a note "Bring a friend, if you have one!" To which Churchill replied, "I'll wait for the second night, if you have one!"

Another comic scene from *Drama at Inish* about the old "fit-up" actors Constance and Hector de la Mare trying to get their "vibrations" right for some Russian tragedy of impenetrable gloom was introduced by a story about the author Lennox Robinson. One sunny afternoon on his way home by tram from the Abbey, Lennox startled his fellow travellers by dashing furiously from seat to seat in an attempt to catch a butterfly. Alarmed for his sanity, a passenger enquired the cause of this commotion. "Don't you know," drawled Lennox, "that a butterfly has only one day of life and I would hate to think that he had spent it on the top of the Dalkey tram."

In the publicity hand-outs for the Oxford Playhouse première, Siobhán described *Here Are Ladies* as "all women as seen through the eyes of Irishmen who don't flatter their women, but who don't flatter themselves either".

A foolish consistency was never a hobgoblin of Siobhán's inventive mind, especially when it came to promoting an image. As if to prove the point, she included Eva Gore Booth's poem to her sister Constance, Countess Markievicz, in prison for her part in the Easter Rising of 1916:

And my own sister, through wild hours of pain,
While murderous bombs were blotting out the stars,
Little I thought I'd see you smile again
As I did yesterday, through prison bars.

Dreamers turned fighters but to find a grave,
Too great for victory, too brave for war!
Would you had dreamed the gentler dream of Maeve,
Peace be with you and love for evermore.[3]

119

The Maeve of those lines, Constance's daughter, later wrote to Siobhán asking her to play the Countess in a play which had been written about her. The work, if it has survived, remains unproduced.

Siobhán was wisely flexible in her choice of material and if she sensed that she were playing to an audience either unsympathetic to or ignorant of Irish revolutionary affairs, she would omit this piece and let Eva Gore Booth's better known "Little Waves of Breffni" wash gently over the heads of the audience.

With another change of headgear, she would strike a *pietà* pose as the Blessed Virgin reciting in Irish "*Caoineadh na dTrí Muire*" ("The Lament of the Three Marys") at the foot of the cross. It was the kind of risk which Siobhán was always prepared to take, relying on her emotional virtuosity to overcome what was unintelligible to many of her audiences.

What might have been regarded as an arbitrary and perhaps idiosyncratic compilation reveals a great deal about Siobhán's deeper insights. While many of the pieces would be known to readers of Irish literature, her selections from the Yeats canon were more eclectic. Few in her audience would have known "The Mermaid's Song":

> A mermaid found a swimming lad
> Picked him for her own,
> Pressed her body to his body,
> Laughed; and plunging down
> Forgot in cruel happiness
> That even lovers drown.[4]

Her "Crazy Jane and the Bishop" sequence was a daring choice for those who only knew the Yeats of the romantic nineties and "The Lake Isle of Innisfree":

> I met the Bishop on the road
> And much said he and I.
> Those breasts are flat and fallen now
> Those veins must soon be dry;
> Live in a heavenly mansion
> Not in some foul sty.[5]

Crazy Jane is the harlot who sacrifices her body on her way to God:

> I had wild Jack for a lover;
> Though like a road

That men pass over
My body makes no moan
But sings on;
All things remain in God.[6]

Her choice of a large chunk of Beckett's *Happy Days*, with the self-centred Winnie up to her neck in a mound of sand, while her docile Willie does her bidding, was Siobhán's sop to bleak modernism. In dialogue stripped of metaphor and music, she now inhabits a world where time, technology, matter, even language itself is running down. This was the precise counterpoint to the second part of her programme, opening with the washerwomen at the ford of Anna Livia Plurabelle. Day has receded into night and the two scrubbers by the Liffeyside are turned into tree and stone. The near pure music of the voices of Shem and Shaun and the lullaby from *Finnegans Wake* is the perfect overture to Molly Bloom's monologue as she waits through the erotic night of 16 June 1904 until the return of her unwanted Ulysses, Leopold Bloom.

This compilation was a personal voyage into the unconscious of Siobhán, the performer, more perilous perhaps than any part she had played. If this kind of solo performance is to be something more than an eclectic and, at times, garish patchwork quilt, a willing if temporary suspension of disbelief is demanded from the audience in return for a sustained sublimation of personality on the part of the actor. Otherwise, as one faces a new audience each night, there is a danger that the known becomes monotonous and the unknown merely bewilders. The carefully matched patterns become a ragbag of dramatic snippets with, at best, a desultory rapport with an audience.

It must have been disquieting for the producers, Wolf Mankowitz and Laurence Harvey, to learn from an Oxford reviewer that on the opening night at the Playhouse their star performer "was still referring to the book in some of her more important items". It would appear that her director had not quite convinced her that her multi-faceted presentation required further work and study on her part.

Although another trial run at Sussex University restored her confidence, it was not without trepidation that she faced a West End opening at the Criterion Theatre in July 1970. It was a theatre mostly frequented by nice old ladies from the Shires, unlikely to appreciate Molly Bloom's lubricity or to enthuse about the indomitable Irishry in the wake of the renewed violence in Northern Ireland. It was also one of the two London theatres flooded by a monsoon thunderstorm in the first week of the limited run.

The first night was one of those well-hyped informal affairs that get media attention:

> I saw only two dinner-jackets. The manager wore one. Peter Sellers wore the other. And Spike Milligan who came with Peter wore a white cotton drill safari and a curious cloth cap. Roman Polanski had a red open-necked shirt. Ringo Starr looked as if he had dressed at the stalls at the cheap end of the Portobello Road.[7]

Laurence Harvey and Wolf Mankowitz could drum up this kind of publicity. There was also an advance release about Siobhán wanting to borrow the four-poster bed in which Winston Churchill was born in Blenheim Palace for her Molly Bloom soliloquy. The Marquis of Blandford said a polite "No – not during the tourist season – they might think Winston was born on the floor." Barry Norman of the *Daily Mail* seemed solicitous: "Perhaps it was just as well. The sound of Molly Bloom's sexual reminiscences coming from such a bed would certainly have offended somebody."[8]

Those who might have been susceptible to such titillation would have been more interested in the advance booking for *Oh! Calcutta*, Ken Tynan's cock-a-snook at prudery with contributions from Beckett, Edna O'Brien, John Lennon and others. In fairness to Beckett, the inclusion of naked figures on stage in his sketch *Breath*, without his approval, infuriated him and led to angry exchanges with Tynan. The shock-value of this hard-core voyeurism did *Here Are Ladies* no artistic harm. On the contrary, Frank Marcus in the *Sunday Telegraph* wrote:

> The immaturity of *Oh! Calcutta* is put in cruel perspective by the vibrant reality of Molly Bloom's incomparable monologue rendered splendidly and with much tossing of hair by Siobhán McKenna ...[9]

Siobhán, in fact, was a pioneer interpreter of Molly Bloom. Nearly twenty years earlier she had made an LP recording of an extract from the monologue for Caedmon Publications in the United States. It was issued, with E.G. Marshall reading from Leopold Bloom's musings on Sandymount Strand, under a discreet sleeve cover of a reproduction of *Peinture Femme d'Eté, 1936* by Miró. It had a rather limited "under the counter" sale in Dublin in the two or three shops which bothered to stock speech recordings. It was certainly a bolder undertaking to include even a slightly abbreviated version in her first one-woman show.

Nowadays, every Bloomsday sees Mollies in varying degrees of undress yes-yes-yessing across the world. But few have mastered the verbal intricacies of her stream of consciousness. The greater challenge, however, for an actor is how to grapple with the polylinguistic rhythms of "Anna Livia Plurabelle". In an explanatory note to this sequence Siobhán tried to convey her personal insights to the average theatregoer, who might be forgiven for thinking that she was once more talking in Irish:

> It is the story of the River Liffey which flows into Dublin City. It is told by two washerwomen. It begins with the washing of clothes in the evening sun. As night is closing in, voices become remote. The women have been changed into a stone and an elm tree. Joyce has put all the things that make a people's inheritance into the telling: landscape, myth and history. It is also full of colloquialisms which make it difficult for the uninitiated to understand. When I was rehearsing it I threw up my hands in despair after five days of concentrated study – I decided the only way was to feel it. The first passage gives us the sight of the river, the second as it is heard and felt ... In "Anna Livia Plurabelle" Joyce plays with words, taking for granted a foreknowledge of place-names and other languages. While this adds to the pleasure of the piece, it does not exclude an enjoyment to be found in the writing for its own sake. One can hear the flow of the water: "She says herself she hardly knows whuon the annals her groveller was, a dynast of Leinster, a wolf of the sea, or what he did how byth he played or how, when, why, where and who offon he jumped her. She was just a young thin pale soft shy slim slip of a thing then, sauntering by silva-moonlake and he was a heavy lurching lie abroad of a Curraghman, making his hay for whose sun to shine on, as tough as the oakwoods (peats be with them!) used to rustic that time down by the dykes of the killing Kildare, for forstfell-foss with a splash across her."[10]

Joyce scholars may cavil at such simple explanations but Siobhán knew *Finnegans Wake* to be one of the great unread books of this century. Her audience, hearing her words undulate like the flow of water, would have to accept that the sound was the meaning. If Modjeska could make an English audience cry by reciting the multi-plication tables in Polish, Siobhán would try to move them to laughter with her voices of Shem and Shaun.

The London critics were eager to share in a new theatrical experi-ence. Irving Wardle in *The Times* wrote of the show as if it were billed as "Mise Éire" or "The Hag of Beara":

Ireland, for reasons that I would like to see fully explained, is traditionally symbolised as a woman. And although she appears in many guises – gallant queen, snaggle-toothed enchantress, the old sow who eats her litter – they are all variations on the two anti-thetical [*sic*] images of the young girl and the hag.

It therefore makes better sense than it would be for other countries to present a stage anthology of Irish womanhood; and no Irish actress is better equipped for the job than Siobhán McKenna who herself possesses the legendary Janus mask; at one moment a thickset potato-faced battleaxe and at the next a seraphic rain-washed country girl ... Even when she launches into old audition pieces like *Saint Joan*'s "Light Your Fire" and Mrs Tancred's elegy from *Juno and the Paycock* Miss McKenna keeps the gas burning low under her rhetoric and cuts through to real feelings. "Where were you," she prays, "when me darlin' son was riddled with bullets?" It was never much of a line; but as she plays it you can see the body lying there with its head in the stream ...

Yeats's Crazy Jane is one that responds most strangely to this treatment; a swooping wild-eyed creature whom you can imagine lurking in the hedgerow ever ready to pounce on the bishop to give him a piece of her mind ...

After the interval, she changes from black to white. First the Shem and Shaun nocturne from *Finnegans Wake*, marvellously responsive to the rhythms, wit and darkening atmosphere. Then Molly Bloom's soliloquy. Molly in fact wraps up most of the ladies that have gone before: if anyone earns the title, she is the Irish woman. And if for nothing else the show is worth visiting for Miss McKenna's classic portrait of her writhing fretfully under the bedclothes in a reverie of petty jealousies, confessional guilts, sexual yearning and everything that makes up her life until she reaches that final ecstatic moment of affirmation. It is a thrilling sound in the theatre.[11]

As she had foreseen, even a critic or two honestly admitted that *Finnegans Wake* was a closed book to them until Siobhán

> turned the choked streams of puns and hybrid words of "Anna Livia Plurabelle" into a note of sheer sound that caresses the ear like the distant Liffey ... "a young thin pale soft shy slim slip of a thing," that wonderful choice of monosyllables.[12]

In contrast to the then notorious nudity of *Oh! Calcutta*, Siobhán, without displacing an inch of Molly's voluminous white nightdress, delivered "a lesson in eroticism by the power of imagination alone."[13]

Some of the tabloids felt that "your mother does really have to come from Ireland if you are to appreciate this pick of the Irish literary pops" but the general consensus was that, particularly in the Joyce section, London had seen a great actress at the height of her powers, in a dramatic mosaic of her own making.

Caryl Brahms in the *Guardian* wrote of

> this great actress who has such a huge range from high tragedy to an early kind of comedy. The National Theatre could do with her. She has her Saint Joan and so does the National. Wouldn't it be a fine sight to see her alternating with Joan Plowright, as once Olivier alternated with Gielgud as Romeo in the New Theatre.
>
> The smoothness of the McKenna voice floating from register to register might set a new vocal standard for Miss Plowright and Miss Maggie Smith.[14]

Siobhán would have had mixed feelings about such generous and well-meant comments, knowing of the jealousy they could arouse in a profession which for intrigue and back-stabbing would make *Othello* read like *Charley's Aunt*. The reactions of the artistic director Sir Laurence Olivier and his wife Joan Plowright to this new planning for the British National Theatre can well be imagined. Anyhow, Siobhán was never invited to play with the British National at either Waterloo or the South Bank.

More surprisingly, the only invitation to play *Here Are Ladies* in Ireland came from the Grove Theatre, Belfast, where she appeared in September 1970, for the benefit of relief aid administered by the inter-denominational Corymeela Community Centre. She said "she wanted to do something for all of the people of Belfast in this time of trouble". She got the usual warnings that most people would walk out if she stood for "God Save the Queen" and that she would be shot if she didn't. She didn't, and nearly two thousand Protestants and Catholics packed the house each night for a week. R.B. Marriott in *The Stage* wrote of

> her grand independence so far as the common rat-race and regular establishment ways were concerned. She has strong loyalties, however, to the tenets of justice and freedom, loyalties in sympathy with the poor and oppressed. In the midst of a popular television programme, when everyone is being artificial, pushful, and silly, she refuses to be anything but her true self, for the sake of higher matters. As when recently, she valiantly gave a famous speech by Juno from *Juno and the Paycock* in the midst of a lot of triviality on late-night television ... She lives in her native Ireland, yet has an international status. She belongs to no clique, or clan or movement of the London Theatre, yet from time to time dominates the West End by the wonder of her performance![16]

Sensing that she could not steer clear just then of an anti-Irish prejudice in theatrical circles, she was glad to accept engagements in the States which her new manager, Milton Goldman, had lined up for her. She also had invitations to appear in Australia and New Zealand. Previously she had turned down an offer to play to segregated audiences in South Africa.

After opening at Joseph Papp's Public Theatre Festival in New York early in 1971, she had to work her way back to Broadway after an exhausting tour of nearly every campus and little theatre from Cambridge, Massachusetts, to the Mark Taper Forum in Los Angeles. These were mainly one-night stands and she travelled from coast to coast with the small crew in a large camper, pulling a trailer with the set and props. There was a guaranteed fee for each performance, but as she moved into the mid-west, audience response varied greatly. In Omaha, Nebraska, there were objections to the title because Crazy Jane and Molly Bloom could not be accepted as ladies of the fashionable kind.

While on tour, Siobhán gave occasional lectures to students at colleges where there were faculties of Anglo-Irish studies. She preferred to describe them as talks, as she hated having to deliver a set script. These "conversations" were off-the-cuff affairs. She liked to tell students of Irish literature that the inspiration for *Here Are Ladies* came from the great copper beech tree at Coole Park, Co. Galway, on which Lady Gregory's distinguished visitors had carved their initials. One feminist wanted to know why she had not included anything by Lady Gregory in her recital, which would be a cue for Siobhán to explain that she had not included other signatories like AE, Douglas Hyde or Jack Yeats either. Denis Johnston once told me an amusing yarn of how Siobhán spoke at such length about Cathleen, the daughter of Houlihan, at some Ivy League college that most of the audience disappeared into the non-Celtic twilight.

A woman student at the College of New Rochelle wrote a lively account of Siobhán on "a day-off":

Siobhán, delayed by a recent stage injury, had arrived late; she is dressed in casual slacks, colourful poncho, and a riveting Indian necklace. Off-stage, the actress, possessed of shimmering eyes, is mobilely attractive; on-stage she is capable of a raving beauty that defies any age but the prime of Molly Bloom.

Siobhán devoted her Monday evening to drama students and enthusiasts. Over dinner, she and a resident chaplain exchanged blarney about eccentric Celtic clergy; the night dwindled into a delicious *mélange* of stage stories told, appropriately, in the little Theater. The actress is a weaver of tales; I suspect some were tall ones, but a collective credulity, so essential in any theater, was accorded to Siobhán that evening. ... Siobhán was reciprocally interested in American student trends and opinions. "Why did McGovern lose?" she asked. "He seemed such a fine and simple man!" One feminist in the crowd questioned her about the dearth of women playwrights and Siobhán, intrigued by the query, later sent the student a note: "Dear Kathleen (ní hUallachaín)," she wrote with a twist of Gaelic, "You asked a very good question. I suggest that you change the answer, write a play!" All of Siobhán's small talk was hugely entertaining and no doubt she could easily have continued far into the morning. ... The campus sponsors of *Here Are Ladies* prepared a small reception for Siobhán after the performance. Students and professors clinked ice in the Board of Trustees room and waited for the guest of honor who was nowhere to be found. Soon word came that Siobhán was on her way. Before gathering kudos and applause, she insisted on sharing her triumph with the girls who worked upon the show. They were backstage sipping Irish whiskey from a porcelain tea cup. That simple dramatic gesture characterizes the generosity and goodness of the life of Siobhán McKenna, the vitality she extended to everybody she met at CNR. ... Siobhán McKenna had brandished such sturdy talent that no one thought to question her relevance to a college campus. It would be like dismissing King Lear because, after all, the main character is ·geriatric and paternalistic![16]

Irish whiskey and Irish history do not mix well and it was fortunate that there were no historians present when she tried to explain the rise of puritanism in Ireland:

I feel it was really Queen Victoria who was responsible. You know it had been forbidden for Catholics to attend university – or when they were permitted, they could not take degrees. So many young Irishmen who wished to be priests had to be educated abroad. Victoria recognised that the English weren't getting anywhere trying to stamp out Catholicism in Ireland. So she founded Maynooth for the training of Irish clergy. And with the new college, the puritanical thing began to develop.[17]

Not surprisingly, such muddled half-truths did not do her any real harm with the more extreme Irish-American societies. She was under constant pressure to appear or perform for Noraid and those who gave support to paramilitary republican groups in Northern Ireland. She refused all such requests. Prior to her appearance in Los Angeles, the writer and former director of the Abbey Theatre, Walter Starkie, emphasised that "she came as a harbinger of peace, not as an amazon of war". Her own explanation was more simple and forthright:

I am not a political person. I'm not for violence. But I want my country free. And I wanted the common people to have their rights ... I thought of joining that march from Belfast to Derry, but my husband was afraid someone might get hurt, possibly trying to defend me. So I didn't go along. But it was terribly moving to hear how they marched all the way, Catholics and Protestants they were, Methodists and Presbyterians came along. And none of them did anything violent. Oh, they were hit by sticks and stones but they never retaliated. This was the greatest thing to happen in the six counties in years and years. Well, I think that scared the politicians in Stormont, Northern Ireland's seat of government. They feared there might be an uprising, a coming together of the common people of both sides, the poor who don't have rights, jobs, or votes. They want to keep these people separate to maintain their power. It's not really a fight between Catholics and Protestants. The poor people on both sides are the victims, of ignorance, of exploitation, and most of all, of fear.[18]

The heartiest applause at the Mark Taper Forum in Los Angeles was for the Irish crone in *The Crock of Gold*, who told her daughter that a woman's vocation was "to hate all men but one and to do your damndest to turn him into a woman too, so you can be boss in the house". But she tells her son that his task is "to hate all women but one and to know how to get around her".[19]

The sound effects were the only irritant:

Miss McKenna has the river in her voice as she plays the Anna Livia Plurabelle sequence ... why bring in a tape of a real babbling brook?[20]

These were strenuous times and her touring manager, Don Draper, sometimes booked her for extra performances at unsuitable venues whenever she had a short break:

I had two days off and they sent me down to Kansas City. I was the only straight act there. I thought it was for professors. There were 2,500 rock and rollers stoned out of their minds – on pot. They laughed at me as I came on (after nineteen blacks dressed up as Indians). I thought I'd walk off or burst into tears but I carried on. They gave me a standing ovation (for courage, not performance). It was freezing down there with snow on the ground.[21]

She was glad to escape to the Australian summer in February 1972. She had developed a "smoky" voice and gave up cigarettes for a short period. After performances at the Perth and Adelaide festivals she played in Melbourne and Sydney under the aegis of the Elizabethan Trust. In a country where Joseph Strick's film of *Ulysses* was banned, there were many who felt that some of Molly Bloom's pelvic puns came a little too near to the *Calcutta* border. For many Australians of Irish descent, their interest in Irish poetry began and ended with "Round the Boree Log". There were, of course, a minority of Joyce scholars, like Clement Semmler of the Australian Broadcasting Corporation, who recognised her as a roving ambassador for Irish culture. Again, the press seemed more interested in her reactions to Northern Ireland affairs:

Softly spoken and feminine, the Irish actress Siobhán McKenna straightened and said, "I don't believe in violence but if I were living in Northern Ireland I probably would become violent."

Intensely Irish in her looks, beliefs and up-bringing, red-haired Miss McKenna was speaking up for the Irish Republican Army.

"I don't approve of the methods they use, but neither do I approve of the British Army shooting down 13 civilians!" Miss McKenna said. ... "It's all very well for me from the South to say I prefer to see a solution brought about peacefully. But when I hear things that are happening in Northern Ireland, my blood boils."[22]

Many of her replies would be unacceptable nowadays to the politically correct, but such sentiments were by no means out of line with the reactions at home after Bloody Sunday in Derry.

Siobhán was apparently cagier with journalists whenever she travelled to Toronto, usually to help Professor Robert O'Driscoll of Saint Michael's College in his untiring efforts to keep an Irish Arts Theatre alive. Many of the critics there were wary of Irish celebrities since Brendan Behan had told them that "Toronto will be a fine town when it is finished." One interviewer there said of Siobhán that "if she ever mastered the knack of answering the specific question asked, she's forgotten it." Perhaps the question was once more about the Northern Ireland "troubles".

The review of her *Here Are Ladies* in the newly built Blair Street Auditorium was wildly enthusiastic in the circumstances:

Lesser artists than Ms McKenna tend to wallow in the limitless capacity of the Irish for self-pity and in their romantic addiction to piddling little religious wars. But this handsome buxom blonde [*sic*] with the flashing eyes, noble features and nimble movements, makes short shrift of mawkish sentiment, plumbing instead the fantastic depths of idyllic poetry and sly humour that condition the temperaments of even the poorest and most uneducated peoples of Erin. ... In five passages from the musings of W.B. Yeats's "Crazy Jane," the stunning power of Ms McKenna in the field of erotica first becomes apparent, especially in the earthy splendour of the poem "What Lively Lad Had Most Pleasured Me". ... As she tosses feverishly in her lonely bed the thoroughly Irish Molly talks to herself about her love-hate relationship with her sensitive Jewish husband and compares these with the emotions that she feels about men she has taken and would like to take as lovers.

These jewels of English prose strung together with seeming random abandon awaken the mind to the breath-taking beauty that may arise from every variety of sexual congress provided the partners are drawn toward each other by forces that transcend simple lust, by love, of course, but perhaps even by affection, compassion or over-whelming curiosity.

Molly even admits that she may even hop into bed with the Pope if God saw fit to give her the chance.

The wholesome candor and shining imagery of Joyce's lines seem to give most people a sense of release from a puritanical imprisonment of the mind. I heard some young men and women close to me gasping with astonishment and delight as Ms McKenna opened the doors, often with echoic and onomatopoeic inflections on her words, to the sunny uplands of thought once closed off from us by shame.

I never heard the Molly Bloom soliloquy delivered with such restrained passion and in such musical English. Indeed, I never want to hear it spoken again by any artist in case Ms McKenna's interpretation becomes blurred in my mind by the odiousness of comparison.[23]

On her visits to Toronto, Siobhán also directed a semi-professional cast in three of Synge's one-act plays at the Irish Arts Theatre and played Juno in *Juno and the Paycock*. In 1973 she returned to London for a production at the Mermaid Theatre of *Juno and the Paycock*, in which Niall Buggy played Johnny Boyle. Sadly, the director Seán Kenny died suddenly and Siobhán had to take his place.

After an absence of sixteen years, she made a triumphal return to New York when *Here Are Ladies*, under the Theodore Mann management, opened at the "Circle in the Square – Joseph E. Levine Theatre" on 29 March 1973. Much has been spoken and written about the butchers of Broadway, especially the *New York Times* critics, a theatrical mafia who for over four decades have spilt much blood on that short strip of asphalt between 42nd Street and Times Square. Rightly or wrongly, individual producers, playwrights and players have had their own particular demon among their numbers. Brooks Atkinson had cast a baleful eye on some of Siobhán's performances in the past. One of the most dreaded of the *New York Times* scribes in the seventies was the Englishman Clive Barnes, now with the *New York Post*. He was ecstatic about Siobhán, recalling her London debut twenty-six years earlier:

Siobhán McKenna – Irish earth-mother and actress – returned to Broadway last night with her one-woman show *Here Are Ladies*! I first saw Miss McKenna when she was a slip of a girl nearly thirty years ago in Paul Vincent Carroll's play *The White Steed* at the London Duchess Theater. Very young, she was a great actress then, and is a great actress still ...

She is a wonderful looking woman. Her face is round and shining, her hair twisted as if by the wind, her eyes glisten with the secret sound of bardic poetry and her voice is low but pure, deep but never husky. She looks and sounds a part of Ireland, and you cannot see her without thinking of Galway Bay or Dublin ...

The Beckett excerpt is from *Happy Days* and Winnie's plaintive optimism in the face of global disaster should not be all that appropriate for full-blooded Miss McKenna. But it is. She brings a special gallantry to her despair that is altogether apt.

But it is for all that in the last section of the program that Miss McKenna really reveals her splendour. Here, she is with that other Irish exile, and Beckett's sometime mentor James Joyce ...

Music is never far away from Irish writing. You can see it even in Shaw and Wilde, while in O'Casey and the poets it runs through the words like the wind of heaven. And with Joyce – almost everything cries out to be read aloud. The printed word is not enough – it is only the score for the orchestration of his language.

Finnegans Wake with its puns and mysteries, its place names and divine gibberish, defies mute reading, and here Miss McKenna, riding high on the swell of theatre, is absolutely superb. But yet Molly's final monologue in *Ulysses*, that hymn to earth, humanity and survival! And suddenly you see that Molly and Winnie might be sisters beneath the skin. Yes, here are ladies. Few of them had an easy life, but they worked with God and nature and made it. It is a rare evening![24]

Richard Watts in the *New York Post*, Douglas Watt of the *Daily News*, and Brendan Gill of the *New Yorker* were equally laudatory, if less flamboyant, in their praise. One television critic spoke of Siobhán as Molly Bloom "fluffing not her lines but her pillows ... At the end clutching a rose to her breast, she seems to fold like a flower at nightfall in time with her whispered 'yes I said yes I will yes.'"[25]

The *Village Voice* summed-up her achievement:

> To be given this kind of insight by an actress is unique in my experience because here in America those of the actors' craft with McKenna's range of experience and professional commitment are perforce shoved into the subtly philistine self-conscious demarcation between popular and "high" culture and are cut off from their resources almost as soon as they have translated their personal anxieties into the terms of their trade. They go insensitive. It is amazing to see an actress of McKenna's toughness whose relations to the serious work of her own culture remain a living thing, and it makes me think, sadly, that probably we inevitably fear culture because we can't recognize ourselves, as the Irish do themselves, as a people. ... What an actress, what a woman! Such luck to have heard her, thank Joyce, as Molly our mother who art in bed, saying her nonsins. See McKenna, for long will it be before you hear again the likes of her![26]

Siobhán could never quite escape the leftovers from the Saint Patrick's Day shenanigans with its shop-soiled green drapery:

> She is a majestic Hibernian queen from the glens and glades of the Emerald Isle and she leads the leprechauns in their wildest dances during the magical hours of moonshine. She is a fighter, too, and she has known her share of Easter rebellions.[27]

It all reads like an overblown description of Maud Gonne or the Countess Markievicz in an American edition of *Ireland's Own*.

It is ironic that Siobhán's imaginative tribute to Irish womanhood was not staged in Dublin until the summer of 1975. A screen adaptation by Sedgemoor Productions had been the British entry for the Venice Film Festival in 1974. It was directed by John Quested and scenes were shot on location at some of Ireland's best-known tourist resorts. It was curious that at the Irish première during the Cork Film Festival, the reel with the Molly Bloom soliloquy was mislaid. Abridged and truncated television versions were shown on the BBC and Radio Telefís Éireann. The failure of any Dublin management to stage *Here Are Ladies* can be partly attributed to the unstinted praise of the overseas antics of Siobhán's Molly Bloom. The annual razzamatazz of Bloomsday was still in its infancy in the early seventies. It was little more than a pub-crawl from Sandycove to Davy Byrne's by a gargle of literary gents, with an obligatory genuflection before the door of Number 7 Eccles Street, which had been re-erected by John Ryan on the first landing of the Bailey restaurant.

Molly Bloom had not yet been accepted as one of the totems of feminism. Joyce, like most of his great contemporaries, was not consciously concerned with the emancipation of women. Siobhán had been criticised by the more militant in the women's movement for her exclusion of women writers from her show. In defence of her virtually all-male choices she replied: "they understood us but they did not flatter us." Nevertheless, Molly eventually was accepted as a spokesperson for the female revolution. But Siobhán gets none of the credit, especially in Dublin, where they had not yet heard her say:

> I don't care what anybody says it'd be much better for the world to be governed by the women in it you wouldn't see women going and killing one another and slaughtering when did you ever see women rolling around drunk like they do or gambling every penny they have and losing it on the horses yes because a woman whatever she does she knows when to stop ...[28]

After four years of her solo marathon in Great Britain, the United States and Australia, she returned to the Dublin stage as the most publicised Irish actress of the modern era. She had still to accept what she always found hard to face after a long absence, the need to reaffirm her position at home. The three-week run of *Here Are Ladies* in June 1975 at the four-hundred seater Gate was a success-ful, but less than triumphal return to Dublin, a city she regarded as the final arbiter of what was most lasting in theatre values.

Much as she was lauded there, Siobhán never set her sights exclu-sively towards the West End or Broadway. Now that she had acquired the status to initiate, and to co-operate on equal terms, her aspiration was to extend the parameters of Irish theatre by exploring the diversity of a distinctive and indigenous culture. She believed one must be truly national to be international. It was a difficult and unrewarding task in a city where the arts were under-funded and where sponsorship was virtually unknown. The Gate production would not have been possible had it not been for an indirect subsidy from the Arts Council, who at that period made the theatre available to outside managements when the Edwards-MacLiammoír company were not in residence. While not prepared to sacrifice herself on the altar of monastic poverty as she did in her early years at the Abbey, she seldom counted the cost when she resolved to do what she thought was important. She had turned down an offer of $100,000 to do television commercials in the States because of her belief that actors are artists who should not be required to lower the dignity of their profession by the insincere endorsement of the efficacy of a certain brand of toothpaste or washing powder. She could not be tempted to take part in Irish soap-operas like *The Riordans* or *Glenroe* even for short runs which would have earned her easy money by Irish standards.

Her notices for *Here Are Ladies* in Dublin were loaded with superlatives, although lacking in any details of the Crazy Jane or Molly Bloom offerings which might startle a censorious sub-editor. That most generous of theatre critics J.J. Finegan wrote:

> Here, then, is a great actress radiant with personality, conveying the essence of each character with surging honesty and complete insight.[29]

All this would be fine, if something like it had not been written about somebody else the month before. It is hard to beat the Dublin critics when they damn not with faint but with fatuous praise.

It was reassuring for Siobhán that some months before she had been officially recognised at home as a roving ambassador for Irish culture or, as she preferred to think of herself, as a *reacaire* or *spailpín fánach*.[30]

Notes

1. James Stephens, "A Woman is a Branchy Tree," *Collected Poems* (Macmillan, 1926) p.72
2. John Locke, "Dawn on the Irish Coast," *Gill's Irish Reciter* (M.H. Gill)
3. Edna Fitzhenry (ed.), *Nineteen Sixteen Anthology* (Browne and Nolan, 1935) p.73
4. *The Variorum Edition of the Poems of W. B. Yeats* (Macmillan, 1957) p.452
5. "Crazy Jane Talks with the Bishop," p.513. Idem.
6. "Crazy Jane on God," p.512. Idem.

7. Barbara Davidson, Darlington *North Echo*, 28 July 1970
8. Barry Norman, *Daily Mail*, 28 July1970
9. Frank Marcus, *Sunday Telegraph*, 2 August 1970
10. Programme note by Siobhán McKenna, Theatre Now Incorporated, n.d.
11. Irving Wardle, *The Times*, 29 July 1970
12. Peter Lewis, *Daily Mail*, 29 July 1970
13. Ibid.
14. Caryl Brahms, *Guardian*, 30 July 1970
15. R.B. Marriott, *The Stage*, September 1970
16. Patricia Lamb, *Campus Newsletter*, College of New Rochelle
17. Interview with Siobhán McKenna, *After Dark*, January 1972
18. Ibid.
19. *Los Angeles Times*, 26 January 1972
20. Ibid.
21. Draft letter to Denis O'Dea.
22. Frances McClean, interview with Siobhán McKenna, *Sydney Morning Herald*, 23 February 1972
23. McKenzie Porter, *Toronto Sun*, 18 January 1973
24. Clive Barnes, *New York Times*, 30 March 1973
25. Donal M. Shoto, WVOX, West Chester, 10 April 1973
26. Martin Washburn, *Village Voice*, 12 April 1973
27. Emory Lewis, drama critic, *The Record*, 30 March 1973
28. James Joyce, *Ulysses, The Corrected Text* (Penguin, 1984) p.640
29. John Finegan, *Evening Herald*, 3 June 1975
30. A poetry reciter or itinerant labourer.

Home to Roost

SIOBHÁN ON OCCASIONS expressed disappointment that Ireland had few honours to bestow on artists. As a professional, she regretted that actors did not qualify for the tax-exemption enjoyed by other artists resident in the state, under the Finance Act, 1969. Nor were they eligible for membership of *Aosdána*, the Irish equivalent of an academy of the arts, which also provides financial assistance to those in need. These were rights which she demanded for professional colleagues at home who earned much less than she did.

Her fellow actors assembled to honour her when she was given life membership of Irish Actors Equity in 1970 and presented with the society's award for her devoted service to the Irish theatre. As chairman of the Abbey Theatre, I was invited to make the presentation at a luncheon in the old Jury's Hotel in Dame Street at which I, perhaps foolishly, spoke impromptu in Irish and English. It was so much "off-the-cuff" that I cannot recall a word I said except that I paraphrased lines from that lovely song "Una Bhán" for the occasion:

A Shiobháin, mar rós i ngairdín thú
's ba choinnleóir óir ar bhórd na banrioghan, thú.

O Siobhán, like a rose in a garden you
like a golden candelabra on a queen's table you.

It must have sounded like a poor imitation of what Christy Mahon had said to her as Pegeen Mike hundreds of times before.

In the following year, the Éire Society of Boston conferred on her their Gold Medal for public service to the arts. Other recipients of this coveted award included John F. Kennedy and the film directors John Ford and John Huston. Over the years, several American universities and colleges granted her honorary degrees in literature and the humanities. In December 1971 an Honorary Doctorate of Letters was conferred on her by Trinity College Dublin. But it was not until 1974 that she made a joyous return to University College Galway, where Cardinal Tomás Ó Fiaich read the citation in Irish at the conferring ceremony. He referred in particular to two of her early performances in the forties, to her Jimín in the first Abbey pantomime, *Muireann agus an Prionnsa*, and to her part in a forgotten play by Brinsley Macnamara, *Marks and Mabel*. These rather esoteric choices may be explained by the fact that the Catholic clergy in Ireland were debarred from attending public performances in the professional theatres up to the late sixties, although they were occasionally smuggled backstage at the Abbey and given a seat in the wings where they could not be seen to transgress any episcopal edict. I have no memories whatsoever of Siobhán's performance in *Marks and Mabel*, which so impressed the Cardinal. Siobhán once recalled that it was in this play she made a fool of herself by failing to check a stage prop, a purse of pound notes, before she made her entrance. When she opened the purse, pieces of crumpled white paper fell on the stage. Next day, a critic pounced on her "amateurishness". She was in a fury.

"We need critics because they are part of us," she said. "I feel that some of them know the theatre and some of them don't know it. But on that occasion, a youth came up to my dressing room the next night. I said, 'What are you doing here?' And he said, 'I wanted to see what you thought of my review. I don't usually cover plays. I usually review hurling matches!' I said, 'Get out of my dressing room.'"[1]

It was ironic that the much-banned novelist Liam O'Flaherty, once an *enfant terrible* of Irish letters, received his Doctorate of Literature at UCG on the same day as Siobhán. The turbulent native-speaking Man of Aran, so seldom seen in Galway, all but upstaged her.

She greatly appreciated the degree conferred on her by the University of Ulster, at Coleraine, as she had campaigned publicly for Derry as a location for that institution.

These scrolls, medals and illuminated addresses were overshadowed when, to the surprise of many, she was appointed a member of the Council of State by the President of Ireland, Cearbhall Ó Dálaigh, in January 1975. She was not the first woman to be appointed to the council, a distinction held by the Cork businesswoman and former senator, Mrs Jane Dowdall, appointed by President de Valera, but she was the first artist.

In conservative political circles there was some "tut-tutting" when it became known that a mere actress, even one of some academic distinction, should be a member of a Council which the president convened from time to time to counsel him on any matter he wished to discuss. A few months earlier, in October 1974, Siobhán had been a speaker at a well-publicised meeting in the Mansion House to protest against the internment without trial of republicans and nationalists in Northern Ireland. The other speakers had included Father Denis Faul of Dungannon, Mary Robinson SC, John Mulcahy, then the editor of *Hibernia*, and Paddy McClean, who had been interned without trial on three previous occasions. According to the *Irish Times* reporter, Eileen O'Brien, the meeting "degenerated into a shouting match" as Provisional IRA speakers prevented the panel from being heard, although they all regarded the practise of internment without trial as an act of tyranny. Like the others on the platform, Siobhán spoke as a democratic republican who in no way supported terrorist violence. Nonetheless, such appearances were viewed with disfavour in government circles and by the professional middle-class establishment, some of whom clung to the old stereotype of actors as "rogues and vagabonds".

When the Price sisters (Dolours and Marion) went on hunger strike in Brixton Prison, in support of their case that they should be allowed to serve their sentences in Northern Ireland, they were subjected to forcible feeding by the prison authorities. In an effort to expose the barbarity of the procedure in which a tube is forced down a prisoner's throat, a public protest was arranged in London in 1974. Several prominent figures, including Siobhán, volunteered to be forcibly fed in public so that more would be made aware of what went on inside prison walls. It was only when Niall Buggy convinced her that the tube was likely to damage her vocal chords irreparably that she desisted, although she continued to campaign until the Price sisters were eventually moved to a Northern Ireland prison.

The president who appointed Siobhán, Cearbhall Ó Dálaigh, was unique among the public men of his era as a patron of the Irish stage. I saw him fifty years ago, when he was Irish editor of the *Irish Press*, taking three steps at a time into the old Peacock Theatre in his haste to be in time for a play. He was a shareholder of the Abbey Theatre up to his appointment as Judge of the Court of Justice of the European Communities. He took a special interest in the work of the theatre and acted on a sub-committee of the shareholders on proposals for amendments to the Articles of Association of the company. No sooner was he installed as President of Ireland in 1974 than he resumed his former role as a regular theatregoer. His visits were not confined to the Peacock and Abbey theatres, where I had, as chairman, the honour to welcome him, but to any theatre great or small where he felt his presence would be an encouragement to a cast, director or playwright. His admiration for performers extended to the circus, which he always regarded as an aspect of show business which crossed all political and language barriers. It was an interest which Siobhán shared. She once appeared as a clown in a celebrity circus, "Circasia", with John Huston as ringmaster, which Kevin McClory, the producer of the James Bond films, presented in the grounds of Straffan House, Co. Kildare.

During one Dublin Theatre Festival in the mid-seventies, President Ó Dálaigh attended three performances of plays on the one day: two at city-centre venues and one at a fringe event in the suburbs. He had one invariable rule: whatever the status of the event, he always insisted on paying for his seats. Never argumentative, nonetheless he was always ready to give a well-reasoned opinion on a play or a performance and to voice it politely and publicly. I recall his fearless comments on Thomas Murphy's *The Sanctuary Lamp*, staged at the Abbey in 1976, which the *Irish Times* critic David Nowlan regarded as "politically important" insofar as it was "the most anti-clerical play ever staged by Ireland's National Theatre". This was enough to raise religious hackles at the time, especially among those who did not bother to see the play. In an open discussion in the auditorium early in the play's run, Cearbhall Ó Dálaigh courageously declared it to be "a play that ranks in the first three of this theatre".

The president and his appointee Siobhán were kindred spirits in that they did not shirk taking a controversial stance on what they regarded as an important issue. Of course, the president's and the Council of State's functions were determined by the constitution and their deliberations were confidential. Ceabhall Ó Dálaigh clearly valued her as an artist who had brought distinction to her profession at home and overseas and found no reason to question the occasional ambiguities of her public utterances.

"I hate politics and don't want to get involved," she announced on her acceptance of a place on the Council of State. "Nevertheless, I will try to do something positive as long as I remain a member of the Council. What I can do, I really don't know yet."[2]

She had actually taken up office during a temporary truce by the Provisional IRA in Northern Ireland after the pre-Christmas 1974 talks in Feakle, Co. Clare, between Protestant church leaders and the IRA. After the break-down of the truce, Siobhán commented that it might have been maintained indefinitely had conditions for IRA prisoners in Portlaoise Prison been improved. She had actually inspected conditions there and, at a subsequent press conference, added:

"We are always talking about the conditions in Long Kesh, but we should put our own house in order, too."[3]

Politics were not mentioned at the luncheon in Áras an Uachtaráin for Micheál MacLiammóir's birthday on 25 October 1975, when Micheál and Hilton Edwards erected little black crosses with their names inscribed in the grounds of the Áras, where the president intended ash saplings to be planted later as part of what he called a Grove of the Muses. At the president's request, Siobhán was present at what might have seemed a funereal occasion, but she was delighted with the idea and toasted its success with Russian champagne.

Siobhán was only summoned to two meetings of the Council of State during the presidency of Cearbhall Ó Dálaigh: one on 10 March 1976, when the Criminal Law Jurisdiction Bill was discussed, and the second fateful meeting on 23 September 1976. After two sessions on that day, when the Emergency Powers Bill, 1976 was discussed in detail, the president decided to refer the bill to the Supreme Court to test its constitutionality. This provoked the infamous reference to the president as "a thundering disgrace" by

the Minister for Defence, Patrick Donegan, at an official army func-
tion at St Columb's Barracks, Mullingar. When the Taoiseach of the
day, Liam Cosgrave, did not ask for the minister's resignation,
President Ó Dálaigh resigned on 22 October 1976, in order to
uphold the dignity of his office as head of state, in whom was vested
the supreme command of the defence forces.

Siobhán went on the RTE news that night to make known her
personal hurt. Next day, she was quoted as saying that "she was
shocked, totally shocked at the news":

> "It's the worst news I have ever heard. This is the worst thing
> that has happened in Ireland that I can remember. President Ó
> Dálaigh had such a tremendous amount before him and we had
> such great expectations.
>
> "At the last meeting on the emergency legislation, he had
> listened to everybody during the four-hour session. I thought
> everybody present was very happy with him. At the meeting
> everybody spoke their minds but afterwards there did not seem to
> be any feeling of dissent with the President, the reverse indeed."[4]

It was typical of Siobhán that she was the only member of the
Council of State prepared to give an immediate reaction about "a
real Irishman". She added: "I think it is very important to nurture
the Irish language, culture, and he is a very cultured man."[5]

Just seventeen months later, Siobhán was to attend the funeral of
Cearbhall Ó Dálaigh in Sneem, Co. Kerry, where he had retired after
his resignation. That day, wrote Siobhán:

> the little village of Sneem was thronged with people from all
> walks of life. Hailstones as well as tears stung the mourners'
> faces. The local people stood grave and silent outside the church
> to leave room for the strangers from Dublin and other foreign
> parts. We had lost a marvellous man. ... He was very much at
> home with us actors as we were with him. He was a genuine and
> frequent theatregoer who liked to discuss the play with us after-
> wards. I remember, during his European appointment, I was
> playing Juno at the Mermaid Theatre in London. My friend Seán
> Kenny had directed me in the part in Toronto previously and was
> to have directed the London production. Seán died tragically on
> the very morning rehearsals were due to begin, and the producer,
> Sir Bernard Miles, insisted that I take over the direction as well as

playing the part of Juno. It was a nerve-wracking experience. Cearbhall read about the production on his way back to Dublin for a visit, and broke his journey in London. It was Sunday. He arrived with his arms full of roses he had bought at a street corner. Afterwards his enthusiasm for the production (we had Seán's set) and his warm praise for the performances did much to console us for the loss of Seán. He was very considerate. I am told that on his first visit to the Peacock Theatre, after he was made President, he was ushered to the President's Box – a group of seats in the left wall, facing out to the audience. He never sat there again, as it was too conspicuous for the actors. I can just imagine having to play in a not-so-hilarious comedy while the audience kept a wary eye out to see if the President was not amused.[6]

Siobhán remained a member of the Council of State under the next president, Dr Patrick Hillery, whom she greatly admired for his gentle tact. Dr Hillery was also a frequent theatregoer but avoided the dramatic gestures of his predecessor. She only attended one meeting during his presidency, when the Private Rented Housing Bill was discussed on 22 December 1981. She continued to take an active interest in public affairs. An early conservationist, she had opposed the demolition of the Georgian houses in Hume Street and joined the protests against the erection of the City Corporation Buildings at Wood Quay. As late as 1986, she publicly protested against Dublin Corporation's plan to build a dual-carriageway outside St Patrick's Cathedral.

Siobhán was prominent among those who attended the Mansion House meetings in 1981 calling for the release of Bobby Sands, who later died on hunger strike. At the unveiling of a sculpture in 1983 to commemorate President Ó Dálaigh in Sneem, she made a public plea for the release of Nicky Kelly, imprisoned for his alleged involvement in the Sallins mail train robbery. She tried unsuccessfully to get Judge Barra Ó Briain, the trial judge, to have the case reconsidered.[7] It was an approach hardly likely to succeed, but Siobhán was never daunted by the prospect of failure if she felt right was on her side. She died before Nicky Kelly was eventually released.

With Ms Evelyn Owens, the *Leas Cathaoirleach* of the Senate, she had represented Ireland during the celebrations for International Women's Year in 1975. Her most publicised participation in international affairs was her address in New York to the United Nations

Special Committee Against Apartheid. On 19 March 1982, in observance of the International Day for the Elimination of Racial Discrimination, she spoke at times discursively, at times eloquently:

> It was as an actor that I first took a stand against *apartheid* many years ago, when together with other members of Actors' Equity, which included such illustrious names as Dame Peggy Ashcroft, we signed a declaration promising never to perform in South Africa until there was an end to their brutal and dehumanising regime.
>
> If we look up the word "equity" in our dictionary, we find that it means the quality of being equal and fair. If we look up the word "apart", we find equivalents such as asunder.
>
> Apartness = aloofness; a part as in French – to a place apart from the general body; separate, separately in thought or consideration; aside; away from all employment.
>
> And thus *apartheid*, based as it is upon the alleged superiority of one race over others, and inseparably linked to man's exploitation of man, is everything which is the opposite of equity... Despite these facts, Irish rugby players accepted an invitation to play in South Africa last year, in the face of a vast turnout of Irish people who marched in protests up and down the country, leaving the players in no doubt as to the feelings and wishes of the majority of our own people. Our President, Dr Hillery, spoke out against the tour, as did our churches, our trade unions, our city corporations, the Government, and other politicians. Private citizens, thousands of men, women and children, marched in a huge throng through the streets of Dublin, ending up outside the Department of Foreign Affairs in St Stephen's Green. I had the task of handing in a letter requesting, as a last resort, that passports be withheld from the players. To do so, we were told, would be a violation of our Constitution which allows freedom of movement to all our citizens.
>
> What an irony of situation?
>
> All the same, it was gratifying to see the great numbers of people who filled the street on this occasion, and I remember the first anti-*apartheid* torchlight procession held in Dublin years before when only about two or three hundred of us walked from the Garden of Remembrance in Parnell Square, through O'Connell Street and ending up then as now in St Stephen's

Green. On that occasion somebody gave me a box to stand on and a few poems to read by African poets with strange-sounding names. As is usual in Dublin, we had a small following of children who chattered away as I read as best I could in a flickering light. It was hardly a captive audience. I could hear a scattering phrase or two from them: "What is she saying?" "Who is she at all? What is she talking about?" Sometimes we must speak out even when we are met with seeming misunderstanding; but I like to think that some of those children at least were among the adults who marched in protest against our rugby players' visit to South Africa. From small springlets come rivers.[5]

In 1983 she lent her support to the campaign against the "Pro-Life" referendum on a constitutional amendment intended to impose further the legal prohibition on abortion. When two of the "Theatre Against the Amendment" committee, Deirdre McQuillan and Nuala Hayes, approached Siobhán for her signature, she invited them to come and discuss the matter. After she had made some amendments to the draft statement for release to the press, she added her name to a long list of actors who were of the view that the amendment "sought to enshrine in the Constitution the teaching of one religious denomination". Despite spirited opposition, the amendment was carried by a substantial majority. The grave reservations of the minority were later justified by the decision in the notorious "X" case and the need for subsequent legislation to rectify the imbalance which the amendment had created.

In 1972 Siobhán had changed house from 23 Highfield Road to Number 40, at the Rathgar end of the same road. Denis had been dealt an unlucky hand in that he was now practically crippled by rheumatism and could no longer drive a car. Siobhán never learned to drive. The new house was nearer the shops and the bookmaker's office. Siobhán had an extension built and arranged a bedroom at garden level so that he would not have to climb stairs or steps. All the furniture, paintings and mementoes were transferred to Number 40, although it was less spacious than Number 23.

During the day, Denis would spend hours in the Gourmet Shop on Rathgar Road, chatting with the proprietor Tom Cronin and the local customers. He was so much at home there that he sometimes sat behind the counter. He was never a man for the pubs and usually rested in the afternoon, especially if he intended to play cards at night. The poker sessions became less frequent and he saw his old friends less often. He was not a total invalid but his illness at this period was a considerable strain on Siobhán's earnings.

Fortunately her great friend Johnny Hippisley helped her to form Quest Productions, a company of which he was producer/manager and Siobhán artistic director. She had known him since the early sixties when he had been a young professional photographer in London. From a theatrical background, Hippisley named the Dublin company after his father who had played juvenile leads in the Liverpool Playhouse and in other repertory theatres under the stage-name Christopher Quest. Johnny's mother, Lindisfarne Hamilton, had also been an actress, but paralysis had ended her stage career when she was still in her twenties. She had a financial interest in the family business in the North of Ireland, Simon Engineering, which still prospers.

Johnny's devotion to Siobhán is unbounded. When I first interviewed him about her in November 1991 he was managing another star, an equine one, the great Desert Orchid, and arranging for public appearances of the retired steeplechaser at racecourses and gymkhanas throughout Great Britain. Although he had little time in Dublin, he rushed away to see Christy Mahon, one of Siobhán's pair of Jack Russell terriers who was lonely since the death of his companion Pegeen Mike. Such posthumous dedication could not be dissembled. He stifled tears at any mention of Siobhán's passing. Thomas Nashe's lines were echoing:

> Brightness falls from the air;
> Queens have died young and fair;
> Dust hath closed Helen's eye;
> I am sick. I must die.

Although Quest Productions staged some interesting plays from the mid-seventies onward, they did no more than break even at the box-office. As a manager, Johnny Hippisley was more than generous in his negotiations with actors. He asked them what they expected to be paid per week and then added an extra tenner to whatever sum they named. "This meant that there was a happy atmosphere even before rehearsals began," he explained. "It was Siobhán's idea that a cast should be one happy family and I went along with that."[9]

Happiness was not enough to make a smash hit of their first production, Noel Coward's *Fallen Angels*, staged at the Gate Theatre in June 1975. This fifty-year-old comedy had in the past attracted the diverse talents of Tallulah Bankhead, Edna Best and the two Hermiones, Gingold and Baddeley. Siobhán was not at ease in the brittle, world-weary sophistication of Coward. William Chappell, a London director with a flair for period comedy, allowed her to appear in slacks with a hairstyle and make-up which seemed a cross between Helena Rubinstein and Nanki-Poo. Siobhán seemed happy that the play marked the return, after a long absence, of Marie Conmee to the Dublin stage in the part of Saunders the maid, in which she moved and sounded like a battleship with all guns blazing. The play ended up, where it might well have begun, at what was then the Liffey Room of the Gresham Hotel, with an improvised stage for dinner theatre. Siobhán was determined that dinner would not spoil the laughs:

"I don't believe in dinner theatre," she announced. "If I want to go out to dinner, I go to dinner; if I want to see a play, I see a play. I don't believe you can combine the two."[10]

Unfortunately, not enough people wanted the play without their dinner and Quest Productions did not repeat the experiment. Most other new companies would probably have got away with the critical response to *Fallen Angels*, but Dublin expected more, perhaps too much, from Siobhán as an impresario.

She set her sights higher when she tackled *A Moon for the Misbegotten*. Because of his Irish ancestry, O'Neill's later plays, which were largely autobiographical or based on family situations, had an obvious appeal for Irish actors. Siobhán would have to convey the protean qualities of Josie Hogan, described by O'Neill as "so oversize ... that she is almost a freak – five foot eleven in her stockings and weighs about one hundred and eighty ... She is more powerful than any but an exceptionally strong man. ... But there is no mannish quality about her. She is all woman."

O'Neill was well aware that it was not the physical dimensions which were important on stage but the psychological hang-ups of this rough-hewn, emotionally deprived woman. Siobhán knew how to portray the animal strength and emotional warmth of Josie Hogan, who is eventually spurned by the dissolute philanderer Jamie – a bitterly sardonic characterisation of the playwright's older brother. A brilliant actor, Denis Brennan was ideally cast in the part, but he had to give it up due to illness. The actor who replaced him at short notice had neither the experience nor temperament for this demanding role. This unsettled Siobhán who tried to compensate by giving another of her bravura performances, which Seamus Kelly of *The Irish Times* described as "a kind of milk and moonshine Pegeen Mike". William Chappell's direction was found wanting. The *Irish Press* notice must have made Siobhán wince:

> Siobhán McKenna as Josie Hogan had an unhappy night. Investing the part with that "full-belt" treatment of hers, she gives us an emigrant Widow Quinn [*sic*].[11]

It seemed that there was no escape for her from her parts in *The Playboy*.

Siobhán was relieved to get an invitation from Tomás MacAnna to return to the Abbey to play Bessie Burgess in a production of *The Plough and the Stars*, which after a Dublin run would tour the States as part of the Bicentennial Celebration of the American Declaration of Independence. The Irish government gave a special grant so that the Abbey could participate. Tomás MacAnna had previously found that Siobhán had reservations about some of the Abbey actors:

> Again she attempted to interfere with the casting, notably wanting Niall Buggy to play a soldier at the end.[12]

She herself would have preferred to play Mrs Gogan, but MacAnna made the right decision in giving the part to Angela Newman. As in *The Cherry Orchard*, her protagonist was once again Cyril Cusack, this time as Fluther Good. The production marked the Golden Jubilee of the play's tempestuous first production in 1926, and played to packed houses at the Abbey and later at the Gaiety Theatre prior to the American tour.

As I was engaged for some lectures on the work of the Abbey at east coast universities and colleges, I travelled with the company and experienced, at first hand, the Abbey's high standing in academic circles in the United States, often in sharp contrast to its reputation at home. This was all the more surprising as the Abbey company had not visited there since 1938. For this very reason, the first preview on 16 November 1976 at the Brooklyn Academy of Music was a tense affair. It is an old and rather ramshackle theatre, seating twelve hundred, on the run-down, rather seedy Lafayette Street. It had been losing money since the war as the surrounding houses became derelict. The once fashionable Hotel Granada across the road had been converted into a home for destitute families. In the early seventies a new management team under Harvey Lichtenstein tried to restore the great days of the Brooklyn Academy, when Caruso, Isadora Duncan and Sarah Bernhardt trod its boards. Annual visits by the Royal Shakespeare Company and an increase in federal subsidies had made it once more one of Brooklyn's showpieces, and the nearby Junior's Restaurant had a regular theatrical clientele. A great deal of goodwill awaited the Abbey company, none of whom were known on the New York stage except Siobhán. Although Cyril Cusack had a European reputation, he was only known to New Yorkers as an excellent film actor, mainly in supporting roles. He had not toured with the Abbey company in 1938.

Lighting miscues, sound tracks which drowned the actors' lines and an American-Irish audience unaccustomed to Dublin accents made the first preview a stressful experience for the cast. Angela Newman as Mrs Gogan and John Kavanagh as the Covey seemed in total rapport with the audience. Cyril and Siobhán, one felt, were keeping something in reserve for the opening night. Cyril told me after the show that he felt that the preview audience were not regular theatregoers and did not know whether to laugh or cry. He was scathing in his criticism of what he regarded as Siobhán's over-emotional dying scene just before the final curtain. In fact, while he waited in the wings to take his curtain, he timed her with the second-hand of his watch on different nights during the run and would say dryly, "Siobhán took two seconds longer tonight before she gave her last gasp." Siobhán, probably knowing how it annoyed him, did not give up the ghost too easily with her dying prayer. Such are the petty vanities of great egos, an essential requirement for great actors. Siobhán, as Bessie, boomed and blustered in a Belfast accent, while Cyril paused and preened. Even the technical mishaps could not knock a flutter out of his Fluther. A distraught Tomás MacAnna said laconically, "I suppose we should be thankful that the set did not fall on top of them."

Fortunately, on the official first night on 17 November 1978, the review of the once-dreaded hit-man of Broadway, Clive Barnes, came to the rescue:

This anniversary, Bicentennial production directed by Tomás MacAnna has been lovingly and beautifully staged. There is a sense of tradition here that enables the play to work with the conscious stylistic confidence of an opera. The actors move around one another with a friendly virtuosity, and the voices blend in with one another, like the cries of seagulls over Galway Bay.

Yes, the Abbey has had its bad times as well as its good times, and I have, for my sins and the pleasures of Dublin, had a few evenings that could, theatrically speaking, be better forgotten. But here they are putting their best foot forward and striding out like a national theater.

Three performances stood out: Cyril Cusack's beautifully modulated Fluther, Angela Newman's deeply felt Mrs Gogan, and, of course, the wonderful Siobhán McKenna, whom I have admired for 30 years now since her performance in Paul Vincent Carroll's *The White Steed*, as the nobly petulant Bessie Burgess.

But all of them were fine in this bold genre study of Dublin – where so much of the action happens off stage, but the Irish rhetoric booms around a properly seedy stage so sensitively set by the designer Bronwyn Casson. And so O'Casey and the Abbey (which rejected him, a decent touch of Irish irony and martyrdom) live again in Brooklyn.[13]

One critic, who had probably attended a preview, reported that "the set for the final act wobbled dangerously, posing for a time a greater threat to Bessie Burgess than Tommie's bullets flying outside her window". He gave the acting honours to Máire O'Neill for "a superb Rosie Redmond".

Douglas Watt in the *Daily News* complained that "the actors seemed to be going their separate ways most of the time, turning the tragic masterpiece into mere vaudeville". He, too, had problems with the Dublin accents: "The brogue gets so thick at times that you fear the whole thing is going to slip into the Gaelic tongue." Martin Gottfried of the *New York Post* found "great chunks of the dialogue incomprehensible. At times the company might as well be speaking Serbo-Croatian."

The adverse comments were wired to Dublin with almost the speed of light while the many favourable reviews were either garbled or ignored.

The Abbey's visit was an assured box-office success; tickets for the New York run had been sold out a month in advance. Although the production had not won unqualified acclaim, a Broadway production company invited the Abbey to return for an eight-week run in January 1977, after they had completed their scheduled tour to Boston, Philadelphia and Washington DC. Before the financial arrangements had been agreed, Siobhán made clear that she was most unhappy about any extension of the tour. She told me she was anxious to get back to Dublin as soon as possible because of Denis's poor health. She said that he had suffered a heart attack and she was greatly upset that she would not be at home for what she feared might be Denis's last Christmas. She also made known that she was more or less committed to play Jocasta in *Sons of Oedipus* at the Greenwich Theatre, London, early in the New Year. She seemed deeply troubled and even suggested that she could easily be replaced in the part of Bessie, which was obviously not the case.

On the other hand, Cyril, who would have dearly loved to play Fluther on Broadway, did not seem to appreciate Siobhán's concern about Denis. His daughter Sorcha was playing Nora Clitheroe and a Broadway date would have helped her career. He could be critical of her work and unnerved her at times by watching her from the wings, especially in her sleep-walking scene in the fourth act. This was in addition to his off-stage activities with his watch to make sure that Siobhán did not break any new records for the longest death scene on stage. Siobhán was not blameless and was extremely naughty when at a gala celebrity concert, which Governor Carey of New York attended, she gave her impression of Fluther in a confab with Mrs Gogan immediately before Cyril went on stage to do his turn. This had been part of her *Here Are Ladies*, but it would have been polite and politic to have dropped it on that occasion. Cyril was greatly annoyed but made his complaints to others hoping they would reach Siobhán.

After the reception that night, he came up to me in the Algonquin Hotel to say that he never saw Siobhán as part of the tradition of the old Abbey company and of the Irish actors who toured the fit-ups with the old Queen's Theatre melodramas of the post-Boucicault era. He usually spoke of her as a great performer and never quite accepted that she was a Broadway star. He would reminisce for hours about "my stepfather, Breffni O'Rorke", Jimmy O'Brien, Ira Allen and other strolling players with whom he had appeared as a child actor. The Fay brothers, May Craig, F.J. McCormick, and even Barry Fitzgerald, according to Cyril, were part of that tradition in which Siobhán could never share.

Dion Boucicault, the actor-manager and purveyor of melodrama, was one of Cyril's heroes. During our stay in New York, he agreed to lay a wreath as a tribute from the Abbey company on the grave of Boucicault in Mount Hope cemetery. We left in a taxi-cab with a news reporter and photographer to find the graveyard, having arranged that the Irish consul and some other members of the company would meet us there with a suitable wreath for the occasion. After a few misdirections, we eventually found the cemetery and the grave, but there was no sign of the rest of the party. We waited impatiently as the darkness fell on a freezing November's evening. The others had lost their way and the wreath. Ever the trouper, Cyril suggested that we should borrow a wreath from a nearby grave for the ceremony. So Cyril was photographed with somebody else's wreath, kneeling at Boucicault's grave while he recited a decade of the rosary in Irish. It was the perfect curtain for a Boucicault melodrama.

"Siobhán," said Cyril curtly, "did not lose her way as she had no intention of turning up in the first place." He was probably right. She knew it was Cyril's day.

When *The Plough* moved to the Shubert Theatre in Boston she was greeted by many old fans when she was a guest speaker at a dinner in honour of the distinguished drama critic Eliot Norton, who had reviewed her performance as Bessie:

> Siobhán McKenna, one of Ireland's great stars, is at the head of this Abbey troupe in a small role ... Miss McKenna gives a heroic performance rich in the music of O'Casey's prose poetry.[14]

Siobhán seems to have believed that she was really "the head of this Abbey troupe", if one is to believe what David Richards of the *Washington Star* reported. He interviewed her later on in the tour in her suite in the Barclay Hotel in Philadelphia.

> "I'm fed up with this tour," [she told him after he had clearly set the scene as a morning after the night before.] "Fed up with it," she says, curling her stockinged feet under her. "There is no way I can possibly answer all the mail for the Abbey Theatre and Siobhán McKenna. The publicity says this is the first tour of the Abbey in thirty-eight years, but I have been coming here regularly for the past twenty years. It's absolutely ridiculous. I want to look after the Abbey Theatre and the Abbey Theatre actors want to look after themselves.

"I've a frightful role to play in all this. I'm not used to working with the company on a regular basis and they're not used to working with me. I'm used to being – well, I won't say spoiled. But I'm used to someone really looking after me. With my one-woman show (*Here Are Ladies*) I have a team working with me and for me. I have nobody looking after me this time. I don't ever want to do this kind of tour ever again."[15]

All the looking after she needed was somebody to keep the safety lock on the door of her hotel suite to save her from predatory journalists. She was a great vulnerable woman who could ramble on and on about the great days of the Abbey like any old trouper:

"I have studied the whole history of the Abbey Theatre," she explains, brushing her hair away from her face. "When they first went to London, the critics were amazed that the actors did not move when they weren't speaking. It was only the actor who was speaking who had the right to move. Some cynics say they didn't move because they didn't know how. But it made an extraordinary impression.

"I still obey that rule. But things have changed. The present company have other ideas; and I can't stand it when people go moochin' and movin' around, mumblin' and bumblin' on someone else's lines. I like sharpness – total, absolute sharpness in a production. I'm not saying the present company isn't good. But it's not *that* hard to live up to the reputation of not movin' on other people's lines. I find that very easy to live up to. There can only be one focus, even in a room.

"I just go mad when other actors put in hems and haws and other words. If you want to put in something the author hasn't put in, put in a silence. You can't go moochin' and movin' ..."[16]

I cannot comment on the other members of the company's immediate reaction, as I was not in Philadelphia or Washington, but I am reliably informed that few took exception to her amazing outburst. She once told Deirdre Purcell that she didn't think that she had ever worked with anyone who didn't want to work with her again.

Mischievously, she says that she is not so sure she can reciprocate the sentiment. "There are one or two now!"[17]

. I have little doubt that Cyril was either the number one or two but I never heard her speak disparagingly about any actor. Cyril was less discreet. Asked by a journalist what was the worst film he ever saw, his instant reply was "Siobhán McKenna in *The Playboy of the Western World*". Johnny Hippisley tells the story, so it is practically certain that Siobhán knew of this devastating comment. Apart from being wildly wide of the mark, it lacked the saving grace of wit. Siobhán could be wickedly funny. When someone wrote of Marie Kean, a fine character actress particularly in lower middle-class parts, as the "first lady" of the Irish theatre, Siobhán purred: "He probably meant the first landlady."

Apart from the rivalry between Cyril and herself and her emotional outpourings to the *Washington Star* reporter, Siobhán made an immense contribution to the success of the tour. She arrived at the theatre early before every performance and, after she had dressed and made-up for her part, she stretched on a couch for at least fifteen minutes before her first call. She would lie motionless, with her eyes closed, oblivious of her surroundings. There is no knowing how she brushed aside the trivia of the day in order to concentrate her mind on her part. She had learned of transcendental meditation from Niall Buggy. There is a curious story that her mantra was *tréis* and that it had something to do with the milking of cows during her childhood holidays on a farm in Co. Longford. At different stages of her life she seemed to become obsessed with farming and cattle, although she would have made an unlikely milkmaid or a "*cailín deas crúite na mbó*".[18]

The tour ended at the Hartke Theatre in Washington DC in the first week of January 1977. It had produced its share of off-stage histrionics and green room tittle-tattle, like all Abbey tours in the States since 1911. While the critics were not unanimous in praise, the audiences, except during the previews in New York, were enthusiastic. Although the return to Broadway, with or without Siobhán, did not get past the discussion stage, the Abbey had upheld its distinctive reputation. Clive Barnes summed up:

> The Abbey has not been in New York since 1938, and it has since then passed through many vicissitudes including a fire that burned down the original theater. But it has always maintained a tradition of acting ... whatever one may think or say about the Abbey Theater, it is very clearly Ireland's national theater. The United

States does not have a national theater, and we can deny that obvious fact until we are red, white and blue in the face but it cannot remove its factuality.[19]

On her return to Dublin, Siobhán must have been reassured about Denis's health. She left almost immediately for rehearsals of *Sons of Oedipus*, a version by David Thompson of *The Phoenician Women* by Euripides at the Greenwich Theatre. Cast as Jocasta in what was really a pageant play, she was meant to be a star attraction in a small unfashionable theatre that was too far down the Thames to set it on fire. Peter Hay in his *Theatrical Anecdotes* has ensured that her performance will not be totally forgotten by including a critic's caustic comment that: "Miss McKenna's voice is exactly half-way between a goose-girl and a whole company of keening mourners."[20]

She was a little luckier in her next choice, *Memoir* by John Murrell, which gave her an opportunity to play in a two-hander with Niall Buggy, with herself as Sarah Bernhardt and Niall as her devoted and fawning factotum, Pitou. It is the kind of piece often described as an actor's play, which usually means that the general public do not show any inclination to share in it. Sarah Bernhardt has always held an irresistible attraction for players like Siobhán, although in her case the only thing they had in common was that they both played *Hamlet*. Siobhán was more of a Duse than a Bernhardt. One did not really believe in Siobhán's version of the little Jewish courtesan who became one of the immortals of the world stage, a self-publicist who slept in her own coffin and who, after the amputation of a leg, hobbled on stage on a wooden peg, at the age of seventy-nine, to the acclaim of thousands, most of whom knew only waiter's French. Siobhán indulged her fantasy as a Parisian prima donna, but those who saw her at the Olympia Theatre, Dublin, and the Ambassador's Theatre, London, and briefly in Canada, saw more of Bernhardt the freak than of "the divine Sarah". As a critic said of another prima donna, Siobhán would have been very good if only she weren't so busy trying to be wonderful. Shaw would probably have liked Siobhán's Bernhardt as it confirmed his worst suspicions of the great French star as

an out-dated ex-actress who left her National Theatre to travel round the world pretending to kill people with hatchets and hatpins – and making heaps of money doing it. ... She paints her ears crimson and allows them to peep enchantingly through a few

loose braids of auburn hair. Every dimple has its dab of pink...
Her lips are like a newly painted pillar box; her cheeks, right up
to the languid lashes, have the bloom and surface of a peach; she
is beautiful with the beauty of her school and entirely inhuman
and increditable [*sic*]... The dress, the title of the play, the order
of the words may vary; but the woman is always the same. She
does not enter into a leading character; she substitutes herself for it.[21]

Niall Buggy was satisfied that *Memoir* was an artistic success. He
had every reason to be pleased with his own performance as the ex-
violinist who made himself indispensable to Bernhardt, only to be
rewarded with screams and tantrums which he willingly accepted
for the privilege of being associated with a great artist. Johnny
Hippisley invested heavily in *Memoir*, but was satisfied that he
broke even. He was an "angel" who never complained when he had
lost money on any venture in which Siobhán was involved. Niall
Buggy was aware that Siobhán had little money to invest in Quest
Productions. She gave it all away, he believed, still paying doctors
bills for actors, sending flowers and champagne to MacLiammóir
when he was recovering from a brain operation and ever ready to
subscribe to any good cause. She did not plan ahead, nor did she like
to be under contract for long runs.

These were the years, according to Buggy, "when she preferred
not to be acting. She would have preferred to direct." She got a
chance to direct when she was invited back to the Greenwich Theatre
by the Artistic Director, Ewan Hooper, to stage her own choice of
one-act Irish plays as part of the Horniman Theatre Season in June
1978. The idea was to mark the achievements of Annie Elizabeth
Frederika Horniman, who had devoted a great deal of her wealth,
inherited from the family tea-business in Manchester, to the building
of the original Abbey Theatre in 1904 and its maintenance until the
end of the decade. An ardent admirer of W.B. Yeats, she had secretly
subsidised the staging of his first play, *The Land of Heart's Desire*,
at the Avenue Theatre, London in 1894, under the management of
Florence Farr. She is said to have arrived at the momentous decision
to build and subsidise a theatre in Ireland by a reading of Tarot
cards and a sudden rise in the value of her shares in the Hudson's Bay
Company. Perhaps as a reminder of Miss Horniman's association
with Yeats in the theosophical society The Order of the Golden
Dawn, Siobhán billed her selection of plays under the general title

"The Golden Cradle". The first part of the programme included *The Rising of the Moon*, by Lady Gregory, followed by two Yeats plays, *The Cat and the Moon* and *Purgatory*. After the interval came another Yeats, *The Pot of Broth,* and the greatest one-act play of this century, *Riders to the Sea*, in which Siobhán played Maurya. T.P. McKenna, Niall Buggy and Kevin Flood headed the all-Irish casts.

A programme of five one-act plays from the early Abbey repertoire had a nostalgic appeal, evoking memories of the company's earliest visits to London when they played at the Queen's Gate Hall, South Kensington, and other little theatres. But it was scarcely a major attraction in 1978, except for American drama students in search of credit marks for their diplomas. As a director, Siobhán adhered to the dictum, "the play's the thing". Far from trying to display her ego, she refrained from any attempt to impose her own ideas about acting on others. "She created," said Niall Buggy, "an atmosphere where acting could become creative." This approach was so far removed from the more dictatorial methods of the directors of the seventies that cynics were convinced that she should not direct at all. She lavished praise on her actors when it was clear to everybody that her own portrayal Maurya in *Riders to the Sea* was the peak performance of that season at Greenwich. Her television performance as Maurya for the Synge centenary in 1971, is of the treasures of the RTE archives

When Denis O'Dea died on 5 November 1978, Siobhán was surprised at the suddenness of his passing. Although it had not been the perfect relationship, her absence at the end made the loss harder to bear. Even his old friends in the theatre and in sporting circles had practically forgotten him, so seldom was he seen in town. After he became more or less totally disabled "he retreated into himself", according to Donnacha, and did not keep in touch with even close friends of former years. As long as he was able, he liked to do good by stealth. In the old days he would drop a pound on the floor of an Abbey dressing room and say to a young impoverished actor, "Take that quid! The fellow that lost it can do without it." When the great tragi-comedienne Maureen Delany suffered a severe stroke, resulting in partial paralysis, he supplemented her pittance of a pension while she lived. Those were the years he played in major films. He could have made a name in Hollywood or in big budget television serials but he preferred to be at home with Donnacha, to play cards, fish and live the life of a retired gentleman. Siobhán once said that nobody really knew Denis O'Dea. In life, as in poker, he kept his cards close to his chest. Even his republicanism was a private matter. He was buried in Mount Jerome with his parents and his Aunt Josephine on 7 November 1978.

Cyril Cusack, the oldest survivor of his contemporaries at the Abbey, wrote of

O'Dea's strong presence on our Abbey stage – a stage in no way second-hand or simply provincially English, in no way derivative from anything but itself. ... he carried the unique quality which this theatre has attracted and engendered ... he stood quietly apart from the abrasive gossip that sometimes affects the theatre and will chip away at the pillars of a small society. He showed loyalty, generosity, and that special humour which is the Dubliner's gift to his city, his city's theatre and to Ireland. He was essentially participant in the kind of work characteristic of genuine Irish acting, reciprocal, communicative and creative – our offering to world theatre – part of a tradition that can never grow old.[23]

I also greatly missed his wry and gentle humour and his capacity for self-effacement, an endearing and uncommon quality in an actor of his standing. He did much to raise the dignity of the acting profession and the reputation of the Abbey at home and overseas.

His prowess at the card table was not forgotten. Gabriel Fallon quoted Seán Lemass as saying jokingly, "Well, take my advice, never play poker with Denis O'Dea. That fellow plays from the cellar up."

The old story went the rounds about the punter who asked, "Who is the best poker player in Ireland?"

"I know that Denis O'Dea is the second best," came the reply.

"But who is the best, then?"

"Anyone who can beat Denis O'Dea," was the answer.

It was more than aleatory justice that the man who could definitely beat Denis was his son Donnacha whom he had introduced to the game. He was placed sixth in the World Series in Las Vegas in 1983 and runner-up in one of the preliminary tournaments. Such reputations, however, are only as good as your last pot. Luckily Donnacha is still a leading player at tournaments in Europe and the United States.

This was a skill that Siobhán wished her son had not inherited. To her thinking, gambling was a more insidious addiction than the smell of grease-paint. She was scarcely aware that the odds invariably favour the professional in betting and in games of chance. More likely she knew that the gambling that is known as show-business tends to despise the business that is known as gambling.

Siobhán mourned Denis's passing in a manner which would have been greatly to his liking: she gave her wholehearted support to the commemoration of the centenary of P.H. Pearse's birth, recording several poems for a special LP produced by Tomás MacAnna for the occasion. The government and the establishment generally adopted an ambivalent attitude to the commemoration, but Siobhán and her "cousin Peig", the historian Dr Margaret MacCurtain of UCD, better known as Sister Benevenuta OP, collaborated in the preparation of a lecture on Pearse and his writings. Sister Benevenuta was and is respected greatly by leaders of the women's movement, and by many radical feminists who would scarcely expect anything good to come out of a convent. This Cork-born Dominican nun's mother was a sister of Professor Eoin McKenna. She had known Siobhán since her childhood and remembers her as "a hoyden with wild hair" when she came to visit the MacCurtains at Listowel, where they lived for a time. By coincidence, it was in Listowel that I chaired their Seamas Wilmott memorial lecture on Pearse during Listowel Writers Week in 1979. Although their vocations in life seemed diametrically opposed, there was a bonding between the pair that went deeper than a family relationship or an intellectual interest in the man called Pearse. At the early hour of 11 am, the hall was packed with visiting students of the writer's craft and, more importantly, by many local people who had taken time off to see the unusual double-act of the nun and the actress.

The main emphasis was on Pearse the educationalist and a discovery of the man behind the myth. The man who wrote *The Murder Machine*, an attack on educational methods, and the founder of Saint Enda's all-Irish school, was as relevant in the seventies as the man who read the Proclamation of the Easter Rising. Sister Benevenuta spoke in the dispassionate tones of the historian, while Siobhán spoke poems like "The Mother" and "The Rebel" with passionate intensity. Sister Benevenuta recalls that in preparation for an earlier lecture in Galway Siobhán would kneel at her bedside at night, head in hands, while she tried to recall Pearse's lines, as if they were litanies.[24]

In many ways, the once cloistered nun was a more advanced

feminist than the worldly wise actress. Siobhán was in the feminist tradition of Countess Markievicz, the first woman elected to the House of Commons, or Maud Gonne. She found it hard to accept that nationalism, of its nature, stifled or stunted feminism. According to Sister Benevenuta, Siobhán was deeply troubled by revisionism or any dilution of the ideals of 1916. With the dethronement of the more romantic archetypes, Siobhán saw no further necessity to tamper with the founding myth of the state. She accepted, however, that there were new forms of reconstructed nationalism which embraced music, drama, poetry and the visual arts. Sister Benevenuta was acutely aware of the deliberate manner in which Siobhán could convey this concept to a wider public:

> "In a genuine and intuitive way, she was in tune with that sensitivity and made a sincere effort to get to the truth behind the myth."[25]

The truth, for Siobhán, was that the state was founded on the ideals of 1916 and that there could be no gain in upsetting the foundations of the state by denigrating the man called Pearse:

Oh wise men, riddle me this; what if the dream come true?
What if the dream come true? and if millions unborn shall dwell
In the house I shaped in my heart, the noble house of my thought.[26]

That noble house could give shelter to ideals as diverse as the socialism of Connolly and the mysticism of Yeats.

Sister Benevenuta respected Siobhán as "a cause person" and as a reconciler in Irish society. Her public activism was part of her ardent nature. She espoused causes – sometimes lost causes – with a missionary zeal. She once told her cousin, then a young Dominican nun, that she herself had thought of entering the convent. This was after a luncheon in Jammet's restaurant in the early fifties when she was a married woman with a young son. "I'll never know that I did the right thing," Siobhán told her impressionable cousin, who found it hard to understand a married woman's struggle between a religious vocation and the stage. Siobhán may have been harking back to the odours of sanctity which enveloped her in St Louis's, Monaghan, where vocations were part of the ethos of the school. Sister Benevenuta believes that Siobhán was interested in the metaphysics of faith, not in any outward show of piety, and that she was never a "do-gooder". Although she was not a feminist in any doctrinaire sense, she showed an interest in the discourse between women and the hierarchy. Although she herself felt "gloriously free", she knew instinctively that the problems of the relations of the sexes could not be solved by an insistence on absolute equality but in a deeper recognition of every individual's right to be different.

Sister Benevenuta, on being asked what Siobhán would have been if she had not been an actress, replied unhesitatingly, "She would have been Reverend Mother of the Saint Louis Order."[27] She had never seen Siobhán on stage except on the lecture tour and on one hot summer's day when she gave a charity performance of *Here Are Ladies* on the UCD campus at Belfield. To a far from captive audience of heterogeneous students, "it was a manifestation of feminism alive". These are some of the special insights of this scholarly nun into Siobhán's spiritual make-up. Beneath the surface of the romantic actress, there was a soft and vulnerable woman who experienced the agony and the ecstasy of her profession. Niall Buggy once spoke of her as "a very non-actressy person", a giver who loved life in all its diversity. He saw her as "a star of life – a shining star of life – who was not consciously aware of her magnetism. She was a star since she was born."

An older nun, her aunt Sister Bonaventura of the Presentation Order, Saint Mary of the Isles, Cork, once, at a family party, put on Siobhán's fur coat so that she could get a sensual feel of glamour and danced in glee. She, too, could get inside the lining of the outward show. She sent Siobhán a note in Irish:

Chruthaí Dia duine speisialta nuair a tháinig tú 'na aigne na mílte mílte bliain ó shoin. [God created a special person when you first entered his mind thousands and thousands of years ago.][28]

She had seen Siobhán in 1974 in one of her infrequent appearances in a television play on RTE, *The Cuckoo Spit*, based on a story by Mary Lavin. She played a middle-aged woman who falls in love with a man nearly twenty years younger than she. There was a bitter-sweet irony in that this delicate, lyrical piece underlined her personal attraction to and for younger men.

Although never a holy Joan, she was always at her ease with priests and nuns. Her "cousin Peig", Sister Benevenuta, knew that if there were the occasional boozy nights, there were also long hours of contemplation and stillness in the dark night of the soul. With glowing humility, this exceptional nun said, "I owe more to Siobhán than she does to me." For contemplation or to study a part, she frequently retired to her hideaway cottage by the sea at Burrow Road, Sutton. She had bought it so that she would be free from the distraction and hurly-burly of Highfield Road.

Donnacha recalls other nights when she would spend hours with a packet of cigarettes and a mug of coffee, on the phone to the States, discussing plays and projects that, at least in the late seventies, did not seem to get off the ground. She was an actress for big parts or big occasions and when the Abbey Theatre was planning its seventy-fifth anniversary programme, Joe Dowling, then Artistic Director, invited her to play Juno in the O'Casey classic which he would direct himself. It was a double celebration which would also mark the centenary of Sean O'Casey's birth. The anniversary night of the opening of the Abbey, 28 December 1979, was a major theatrical occasion. For the first time a President of Ireland made a speech from the stage in praise of the theatre's achievements and its capacity for survival against what, at times, had seemed insuperable odds. Joe Dowling introduced the president and I spoke some words of thanks and appreciation. These speeches were before the performance, as we feared that if the president spoke after the performance, there might be an unseemly rush from some parts of the house to the pubs or to the reception planned at a nearby venue. As chairman, I felt that I should not only pay tribute to the players and staff of the new Abbey, but also ask the audience to give a round of applause to the long line of Abbey actors and playwrights who had made their last exit from life's stage: there was a tumultuous response from the invited audience. Although she had not heard the speeches, Siobhán heard the applause. She told me that the speeches should have been given after the show as the delay had added unnecessarily to the first night nerves of several members of the cast. The arrangement did not worry Joe Dowling, who was directing his first major production of an O'Casey play. Siobhán seemed satisfied with his approach to the play which was exploratory and assured. However, it did not scale the heights he later reached with what critics hailed as his definitive Juno – a somewhat terminal description – staged at the Gate Theatre and in London and New York in the mid-eighties.

Siobhán did not seem to be acting on her nerves. She had settled into the part of Juno in several performances since she had first played it with Peter O'Toole at the Gaiety in 1966. She had become a larger-than-life figure and dominated in every scene, with her noble head held high and with the walk of a tenement queen. Joxer (Eamon Morrissey) and Captain Boyle (Philip O'Flynn) were intent on wringing the last drop of emotion and the last chuckle of ironic laughter from the tragi-comedy but they were confronted with a personality performance that overwhelmed them. O'Casey's women are of heroic mould, his men of weaker fibre. Lennox Robinson described Sara Allgood's first Juno as "grandiose", an epithet which fitted what was to be Siobhán's last Juno in everything except Allgood's mastery of the Dublin dialect. In this respect, it fell short of greatness. Even the greatest of stage stars cannot excel in every production. There is a story that Mrs Patrick Campbell while rehearsing Yeats's *Deirdre* asked the poet what he thought of her performance. "I was thinking," said Yeats, "of an Indian station master in a remote village who phoned the terminus to say that there was a tigress on the line and asked 'what can I do?'"

Directors can have problems when actresses of the calibre of Mrs Campbell or Siobhán break loose.

Notes

1. Donnacha Ó Dulaing, *Voices of Ireland* (O'Brien Press, 1985) p.185
2. *Irish Times*, 17 November 1986
3. Ibid.
4. *Irish Press*, 23 October 1976
5. Ibid.
6. Siobhán McKenna, *Some Recollections on Cearbhall Ó Dálaigh*, unpublished typescript; Aidan Carl Matthews (ed.), *The Immediate Man* (Dolmen Press, 1983) pp.73, 75
7. Interview with Siobhán's cousin, Sister Benevenuta, UCD, November 1993
8. Extract from United Nations Press Release, 22 March 1982. Department of Political and Security Council Affairs.
9. Interview with Johnny Hippisley, November 1991
10. Gus Smith, interview with Siobhán McKenna, *Sunday Independent*, 6 July 1975
11. Phillip Molloy, "Misbegotten at Gate," *Irish Press*, 17 June 1976
12. Unpublished notes to the author, January 1993
13. Clive Barnes, *New York Times*, 18 November 1976
14. Eliot Norton, *Boston Herald American*, 1 December 1976
15. David Richards, *Washington Star*, 19 December 1976

16. Ibid.
17. Deirdre Purcell, interview with Siobhán McKenna, *Sunday Tribune*, 23 November 1986
18. Pretty girl milking the cows; Bríd Mahon, interview with Siobhán McKenna, *Irish Press*
19. Clive Barnes, *New York Times*, 8 December 1976
20. Peter Hay, *Theatrical Anecdotes* (Oxford University Press, 1987) p.274
21. George Bernard Shaw, *Dramatic Opinions and Essays*, vol. I (Constable, 1907) pp.135-36
22. Interview with Niall Buggy, March 1993
23. Cyril Cusack, "An Appreciation," *Irish Times*, 11 November 1978
24. Interview with Sister Benevenuta OP, December 1993
25. Ibid.
26. P.H. Pearse, "The Fool," *Plays, Stories & Poems* (Talbot Press, 1963)
27. Sister Benevenuta, op. cit.
28. Note to Siobhán from Sister Bonaventura, Cork, n.d. circa 1971

Swan Song

NOW THAT SHE had passed the meridian of her career, Siobhán was regarded in some circles as not so much the *grande dame* as the Celtic matriarch of the Irish stage. A new generation drew a distinction between the leading actress of at least three decades and the public campaigner for civil rights and individual freedom. She was also a patron of the National Children's Theatre and co-operated with Dame Ruth King and others in an effort to foster the stage involvement of young people. She had developed a multi-layered personality and saw no reason to change it to suit the whims of radical *chic*. Indeed, she found little to attract her in the social realism of many of the plays which brought new life to the Peacock, the Project and other little theatres in the seventies. There were few parts big enough for her matriarchal eminence. And there were young theatregoers and critics who were slow to accept that anybody should be acclaimed a star for so long. Youth always finds it easy to knock idols from their pedestals.

Siobhán was fortunate that her loyal friend Johnny Hippisley and Quest Productions were still around to make it possible for her to tour again on the Continent. As far back as 1974 she had played excerpts from *Here Are Ladies* in Brussels before the King and Queen of Belgium during the state visit of President Childers to that country. In 1979 Quest Productions presented *Here Are Ladies* in Vienna's English Theatre, then the only professional theatre in

Europe staging works in English on a regular basis. An Austrian critic wrote that

> An Irish whirlwind, a natural force of a woman is performing solo at Vienna's English Theatre. Siobhán McKenna is not young and is not beautiful by the usual standards, but she fascinates – she puts her audience progressively more and more under her spell. She speaks texts by Irish poets, begins somewhat conventionally, builds up to a great intensity and ends with the famous thoughts of Molly Bloom – a sensation.
>
> Not only must one hear Siobhán McKenna, one must also see her. She speaks not only with her voice but with her entire body and above all with her magnificently expressive face.
>
> This face is that of a landscape.[1]

Quest Productions were invited back to Vienna in 1980 for a co-production by Franz Schrafanek and John Hippisley of *The Shadow of a Gunman* for the O'Casey centenary. It was perhaps Siobhán's best work as a director. She also played the small but rewarding part of Mrs Grigson with a fine cast which included John Molloy as Seamus Shields, Niall Buggy as Donal Davoren and Philip O'Flynn as Adolphus Grigson. Apart from Siobhán's solo performance, this was the first production by an Irish company in Vienna's English Theatre. The *Kurier* review told its readers:

> Let us forget everything we have been served with over the last few years as O'Casey's regardless of the stage where it was presented. Never have they succeeded in doing justice to the Irish dramatist, his Irish humour and sufferings, his dramatic art so full of spirit and tragedy. What was lacking until now was a standard of comparison to measure these productions. Now we have a reference point: Siobhán McKenna's *Gunman*. This production unmasks the others.[2]

In 1981 she tried once more to match strides with Sarah Bernhardt when she appeared in one of the French star's favourite rôles as Agrippina in *Britannicus* at the Lyric Theatre, Hammersmith. Never likely to permit chivalry to obscure criticism, the Francophiles among the audience gave a mixed reception to a brave but ill-timed effort to recapture past glories.

Siobhán's return to the Abbey Theatre for the Joyce centenary in *Joyce Women* in June 1982, where she played Molly Bloom for the last time, was a great and popular triumph. In her sixtieth year, enfolded in a voluminous white night-dress, enthroned on the feather bed, she had to battle for supremacy, as rival Mollies not half her age gave full blast to their fantasies in playhouses, pubs and public parks.

The only rival who really mattered was the younger and radiant Fionnuala Flanagan at the Gate Theatre in a stage version with an acceptable display of nudity. At least two video recordings were made of her captivating performance. One was a sanitised, fully covered version for home consumption, but there was a steamier and more explicit video made for distribution abroad and for parties in Dublin 4, likely to raise goose-flesh on Joyce. Siobhán seemed unconcerned at the ubiquity of the competition. From early morning on Bloomsday 1982, RTE radio broadcast an uncut reading of the text that continued until noon the following day. There were Joyce students and scholars everywhere. They were overwhelmed at the Abbey as the waves of Molly's sensuality washed over them, with an exact measure of emotion and vocal mastery.

Over the years, she continued to supplement her income by occasional appearances in television plays like Edna O'Brien's *A Cheap Bunch of Nice Flowers* and *The Diary of Brigid Hitler*, in which she played the part of the alleged Irish sister-in-law of Hitler. Her stage appearance at the Gaiety Theatre in 1985 as Abby Brewster, one of the "pixielated" old ladies in *Arsenic and Old Lace*, was an entertaining "lark" with her good friend Maureen Potter, who had been impersonating her for thirty years.

She had faced a much greater challenge in February 1984 when she agreed to play one of the most demanding parts in modern theatre, that of Mary Tyrone, in a revival of *Long Day's Journey Into Night* at the Abbey Theatre. Earlier Abbey productions of O'Neill's posthumous masterpiece had earned plaudits for Ria Mooney in 1959 and 1962, and for Angela Newman in 1967. Ria Mooney's performance, particularly in the 1962 revival, was the greatest in her career and the most discussed since her Rosie Redmond in the original production of *The Plough and the Stars* in 1926. Frank Dermody's earlier productions had met, to the last comma, Mrs Carlotta O'Neill's stipulation that the play should be played uncut as written. It was also a recognition by the Abbey that O'Neill had accepted an invitation by Yeats to become an associate member of the Irish Academy of Letters. Philip O'Flynn, T.P. McKenna and Vincent Dowling combined excellently with Ria

Mooney to make the earlier productions highlights of the Abbey's rather dim sojourn at the Queen's Theatre from 1951 to 1966, after the disastrous fire.

In the world première of the play at the Royal Theatre, Stockholm, and in the first Broadway production of 1956, the main focus of the play was on the father, James Tyrone. In José Quintero's Broadway production, Frederic March was at the very centre of the play as the matinée idol James Tyrone, overshadowing the performance of Florence Eldridge as his drug-addicted wife, Mary. Later Irish actresses like Geraldine Fitzgerald in New York and Ria Mooney in Dublin added new dimensions to the role of Mary Tyrone. In the 1985 Abbey production, Siobhán found that she could identify with the part to an even greater degree than her distinguished predecessors.

The director, Pat Laffan, who had played an appropriately dissolute James Tyrone in the 1967 Abbey production, enthused about Siobhán's performance:

> Siobhán was magnificent, perfectly in tune with the part; when she spoke that final line ("I fell in love with James Tyrone and was so happy for a time") in rehearsal, I just broke down. She wanted to do the part. She had it thoroughly researched. She knew what to do about the hands and had looked into the effects of the drug. She had someone send for a foghorn on tape, which we used. We tried to be authentic all the way. She and I decided to observe all the stage directions. We had a very classical set: Grecian appropriate to tragedy.[3]

Pat Laffan implies that Siobhán, with his agreement, had taken on the role of co-director. Now Godfrey Quigley as James Tyrone was no longer centre stage, unlike Frederic March, Sir Laurence Olivier, Jason Robards and Anew McMaster who had all played the part in previous productions.

As was her custom whenever she wanted to concentrate and memorise a major part, she went away to her cottage in Sutton. As she studied the part, she found a great deal in the character of Mary Tyrone with which she could empathise – her convent upbringing and her suppressed longings to take the veil. Siobhán saw much more in the part than a pitiful object of sympathy who wandered about in a drug-induced haze of indecision and recrimination. There was a whiff of sulphur in the saintly air of martyrdom which drove

Mary Tyrone's family to the edge of despair. In this production, Siobhán became the pace-setter, making Mary Tyrone the centre-piece of the tragedy. Godfrey Quigley as her husband James Tyrone and Desmond Cave and Stephen Brennan as her sons responded admirably to her mood changes but the production as a whole seemed out of kilter. The playwright's intention was to show that each member of the doomed quartet had a share in the family guilt. Siobhán's dominance made it too easy to blame Mary Tyrone.

The audience and some critics were lukewarm in their response and Siobhán was particularly sensitive to the implication that she failed to capture O'Neill's almost obsessive preoccupation with his Irish ancestry. The prototype of Mary Tyrone, Ella Quinlan, the playwright's mother, had spent a great deal of her life trying to avoid being labelled shanty Irish, like the post-Famine emigrants of whom her husband-to-be James O'Neill (Tyrone) was a prime specimen. He had had to get rid of a peasant brogue and the harum-scarum image of the happy-go-lucky stage-Irishman, which had been eminently suitable for the Boucicault melodramas in which he appeared as a young actor, but were scarcely the most appropriate training for an actor who later boasted that he had played Iago to Edwin Booth's Othello. However, he abandoned what promised to be a great career as a Shakespearean actor to become a matinée idol in seemingly endless tours of *The Count of Monte Cristo*. Siobhán was well aware that the playwright's mother, Ella Quinlan, had greatly diluted the strong brew of her Irishness. She, too, was the child of post-Famine emigrants who had prospered in the grocery trade and in real estate dealings. Her upbringing was that of the convent-educated daughter of a highly conventional Catholic home. She was "lace-curtain Irish", who were often slightly ashamed of their Irishness, now that their brothers and sons were distinguishing themselves at Harvard and Yale. The O'Neills could never quite rid themselves of the description "shanty Irish" and remained suspi-cious of their more ambitious and successful compatriots, who were aping their Yankee betters.

Siobhán was also aware of the darker side of O'Neill's Irishness and in her portrayal of Mary Tyrone showed the will for self-destruction at war with the search for redemption. The Irish reluc-tance to face grim reality, the pipe-dreams of *Tír na nÓg*, the search for a Land of the Blest, were explicit in her interpretation. Unfortunately, the length of the unrelieved tragedy and a lack of cohesion in the ensemble playing resulted in a mixed response to what was the least financially successful of the four Abbey productions of the play.

Her last association with the Abbey was as director of her own stage arrangement of *Cúirt an Mheán Óiche* (*The Midnight Court*) in October 1984. Siobhán's deep insight into the rhythm and vigour of Merriman's eighteenth-century epic poem was reflected in her direction, with costumes and design by Wendy Shea and music by Donal Lunny. Although several stage versions in English had been seen, this was the first in the original Irish. Actors with the skills and fluency of Bríd Ní Neachtain, Maíre Ní Ghráinne, Peadar Ó Luain, Macdara Ó Fatharta and Micheál Ó Briain rallied around Siobhán in what was to be her last hurrah at the National Theatre. There was an excellent response from the audience and critics. *The Irish Times* reported:

> If poetry is notoriously difficult to translate to the stage, then the thousand lines of Brian Merriman's bawdy 18th-century epic, in archaic Irish, must have presented exceptional problems. Siobhán McKenna's adaptation at the Peacock overcame them all. Boring recitation was avoided through the vibrant performances of the cast and the music of Donal Ó Luinigh, and the general atmosphere was one of a great ribald romp, a large slice of the "crack" with its serious side as well.
>
> There are telling satirical blows for women's lib written at a time long before that concept was given a formal title and still relevant today. The old bachelor farmers of Munster have their sexual deficiencies exposed by Bríd Ní Neachtain who as the Spéirbhean, Una, gives a splendid performance, flitting along the tongue-twisting litany of adjectives attached almost to every noun and expertly portraying the character of a woman who could be described in today's English gossip columns as "fun-loving" or extremely vivacious.
>
> There is none of that sort of understatement in the poem itself as the sexual abilities of the older men are compared to those of their younger brethren with an explicitness of detail that would make Jackie Collins blush.[4]

The only dissident voice was that of the lively controversionalist Fintan O'Toole in the *Sunday Tribune* under the headline "Anodyne Erse":

In its original version, as spoken here, *Cúirt an Mheán Óiche* is dense and difficult, accessible to what can only be a small minority even of Irish speakers. Yet no attempt is made by Siobhán McKenna to create theatrical images around the poem in a way that might bring it to life with visual or physical impact. Not only does this make for a dull and one-dimensional piece of theatre, it also produces a travesty of Merriman's spirit.

The Midnight Court is a poem primarily about sex. To transfer it to the stage should imply at least some sense of a physical language, a language of touch and presence. In Ms McKenna's version it is alright to use Merriman's dirty words (since after all only refined and cultured people will be able to understand them in the original) but it is not at all right to *do* anything dirty since then everybody would have some idea of what might be going on. Hardly ever does anyone on stage touch anyone else.

Apart from the element of travesty in this, it also makes for a rigidly static piece of theatre. Most of the actors spend most of the time rooted to the spot enunciating the verse. It is significant that the best and funniest performance comes from Maeliosa Stafford who has hardly any lines whatever and therefore presumably had to invent a performance for himself. Only Wendy Shea's costumes and Bríd Ní Neachtain's singing provide any occasional sense of excitement.[5]

This critic seemed to be obsessed by the startlingly novel idea that a verse play would greatly benefit if there were little or no verse in it, at least if it was written in an inaccessible language like Greek or Irish. He fails to explain how a dramatic *aisling* or vision poem can be reduced to some kind of mummer's mime or sexual acrobatics. Song, dance and music were the appropriate embroideries for the vital and extravagant speech of Merriman. There was certainly a place for it in Yeats's theatre:

The bastard's speech in *Lear* is floating through his [Merriman's] mind, mixed up no doubt with old stories of Diarmuid's and Cuchulain's loves and old dialogues where Oisín railed at Patrick, but there was something more, an air of personal conviction that was of his age, something that makes his words – spoken to the audience – more than the last say of Irish paganism. ... The girl replies to the old man that if he were not so old and crazed she would break his bones, and that if his wife is unfaithful what

171

better could he expect seeing that she was starved into marrying him. However, she has her own solution. Let all the handsome young priests be compelled to marry. Then Eivell of Craglee gives her judgment, the priests are left to the Pope who will order them into marriage one of these days, but let all other young men marry or be stripped and beaten by her spirits. The poem ends by the girl falling upon the poet and beating him because he is unmarried. He is ugly and humped, she says, but might look as well as another in the dark.[6]

This was how it was staged in Siobhán's version. She could scarcely be expected to reduce a discussion about clerical celibacy to some kind of theatrical semaphore. Anyhow, if Merriman's poem is primarily about sex, it is about sex in the dark.

Siobhán once told her friend Eibhlín Ní Bhriain of *The Irish Times* that if she were to play a part in her stage version of *Cúirt an Mheán Óiche*, it would not be that of the traditional *spéirbhean,*

A pleasing, teasing and tempting tart
That might coax and entice the coldest heart!

She would opt for the part of the bleary-eyed harridan who drives the slumbering poet astray in his wits:

I threw a glance with beglamoured eyes
And beheld a hag of hideous disguise,
Her shape with age and ague shook
The plain she scoured with slavering look,
Her girth was huge, her height was quite
Seven yards or more if I reckoned it right,
Her cloak's tail trailed a perch's length,
She gripped a staff with manful strength,
Her aspect stark with angry stare
Her features tanned by wind and air,
Her rheumy eyes were red and blear,
Her mouth was stretched from ear to ear.[7]

The above, allowing for the Gaelic propensity for exaggeration and caricature, is a reasonably accurate pen-picture of what Siobhán would look like in her last and perhaps greatest triumph as Mommo in *Bailegangaire* by her friend Tom Murphy. Although she must have known him for over twenty years, she had never appeared in a play by Murphy, one of Ireland's major playwrights and a Galwayman for good measure. He had given up his job as a metal-work teacher in Mountbellew, near his native Tuam, to become a full-time playwright of unique distinction. With characteristic courage and integrity, he became writer-in-association from 1983 to 1985 with the tiny Druid Theatre, which seated little more than a hundred, in Chapel Lane in Galway City. Largely due to the creativity of its Artistic Director, Garry Hynes, it had within ten years won a well-deserved reputation as an innovative force in Irish theatre. But its founders must have counted their blessings when Siobhán returned to Galway to rehearse for the most important première in the Druid's first decade. Tom Murphy had made clear that he had written the part of Mommo in *Bailegangaire* with Siobhán in mind, but the little theatres of the world are paved with high ambitions to attract star billings. Siobhán was forthcoming and down-to-earth about her appearance with Druid:

Tom Murphy had said he had written the part of Mommo for me, but that the play itself was for Druid. I think this was a very happy marriage because there is no other place in which the play should have started, not only because it is set in the west of Ireland, but also because Druid have a primitive approach to a play from the roots up. I admire that and I think that *Bailegangaire* is getting an attention, a focus, that it might not have received in a more commercially minded theatre ... I don't want to put people off but there are times when I have seven pages of dialogue non-stop! But Mommo is acting out many different characters then, not just describing things. There's also a great deal of humour, explosive bursts of comedy in the most unexpected places. But then Irish people cry at weddings and get the giggles at funerals, because the most extreme emotions are still tied up together. So it's all in keeping with that.[8]

Even before the play had opened, Siobhán was generous in her praise of her two collaborators in this play for three women, with a woman director to complete the quartet:

Marie [Mullen] is a beautifully instinctive actress and a very caring one. Mary [MacEvoy] proved her commitment to the play early on, when she was still doing *Glenroe*, by driving down from Wicklow every evening for rehearsals, then driving back at dawn for filming. Garry [Hynes] is very much at the root of the play. She gets a conception, but she's not dictatorial about its interpretation. She'll have a vision of the play, and then sometimes she'll say, "I don't know. I don't see. Let's think together."

You know, at that moment, we four women, we're like a family of old recluses! We go up that ladder of the rehearsal room, and we bang down that trap door and there we are with no one but ourselves. I hadn't thought about it until the other day, when it struck me as quite unusual that we are just four women in a room, working, working, working, together – and having a lot of laughs.[9]

Tom Murphy did not originally intend to write *Bailegangaire* as a three-hander for women. In an earlier version there was a male character but, as the author put it, "a play dictates itself and its characters dictate themselves". There is no straightforward plot development such as one expects in a conventional play. Mommo, a senile old woman in her eighties, tries to exorcise the demons of her past by telling her two granddaughters, whom she doesn't even recognise, a seemingly endless story, which she repeats each night but refuses to finish. Murphy's interest is in the complexity and contradictions of his characters. In a revealing interview with Ciaran Carty in the *Sunday Tribune*, he explained:

She [Mommo] has a compulsion to tell her story and yet a fear of it. As if distancing herself from the experience, she remembers it in the third person.

The three women are at war, and yet at the same time dependent on one another. They are very different and yet they form a kind of unity.[10]

The traditional single setting of a thatched cottage, excellently designed by Frank Conway, was deliberately stylised so as "to avoid cliché". Commenting on what technology had done for the west of Ireland, the playwright points out the incongruities:

You can have a man up to his knees in turf tuned into a Walkman. Perhaps a helicopter flies overhead with Tony O'Reilly. Down the road people are watching *Dallas* in a pub. Or maybe there's a computer factory. Part of the background of the play is showing these anomalies while the drama is going on in a thatched cottage.[11]

In the thatched cottage, Siobhán as Mommo had to wrestle not only with past demons but with reams of dialogue, until she was nearly exhausted. Niall Buggy flew over from London to help her learn her lines. He now believes that she was unwell, and that "she did all *Bailegangaire* on one lung and long speeches on one breath".[12] She did not complain.

On the opening night on 5 December 1985 she gave the kind of performance that Galway had not seen since her *San Siobhán* thirty-five years earlier. Throughout the play Mommo is confined to a double-bed in the kitchen – the warmest room in the house – except when she rises once to sit on the chamber-pot. In her nightly discourse on the unfinished saga of the misfortunes of Bailegangaire (the town-land of no laughter), she grapples with the intricacies and complexities of a seemingly unending folktale that is a patchwork of guilt and ultimate redemption. It was a heartbreaking but warmly human performance. The Celtic matriarch, no longer rich and rare like the gems she wore, had transformed herself into the Hag of Beara:

I am the old woman of Beara
An ever-new smock I used to wear
To-day, such is my mean estate
I wear not even a cast-off shift.
I see upon my cloak the hair of old age,
My reason has beguiled me:
Grey is my hair that grows through my skin
Tis thus! I am an old woman.[13]

Not only an old woman but a mad woman, who in a momentary flash of lucidity at the play's end finishes a horrendous story that releases her from the past and gives a glimmer of hope for the future to her two granddaughters.

The local and national papers carried rave notices. Even the previously sceptical Fintan O'Toole became a convert to the Siobhán cult:

Siobhán McKenna emerges in *Bailegangaire*, as she has not done in Ireland in recent years, as a great actress. Her grand style and the amazing range of her voice work here not as mere display, but as a superbly disciplined and well-aimed performance. The scale of her style, the fact that Mother Ireland hovers in the background of her stage persona, is exactly right here, precisely because she is, in one dimension of Mommo, Mother Ireland. But it is not the Mother Ireland of long and noble suffering, weeping and wailing. It is a Mother Ireland who spits and urinates.

Siobhán McKenna here is foul, terrifying and insidious, as well as being somehow haunting and ultimately very moving. She makes herself at times physically ugly, setting her face in a hard mannish expression that will melt only when the moment of resolution is reached. It is a performance of rare stature.[14]

The novelist and critic, Colm Toibín, also struck the right note with a top C.

The story of *Bailegangaire* is fixed and imprisoned in the mind of Mommo (Siobhán McKenna). She reels the story out over and over again as though it were a prayer or a magic spell. In the end it becomes both ... The great moment in the play, which Siobhán McKenna has beautifully built the audience up to, is the end of the story, told with a brutality and hardness, savage in its implications, heart-rending for an audience.

Afterwards, which is where the play's greatness lies, comes the possibility of love and a new start.

Siobhán McKenna is just extraordinary. She acts, using her mouth and eyes with incredible skill, a part in which she is utterly convincing.[15]

Siobhán, despite Niall Buggy's forebodings, seemed genuinely happy to be back in Galway. During the rehearsals and the run of the play, both before Christmas – which she spent in Dublin – and for another three weeks' run in January 1986, she did not smoke or drink. She renewed acquaintances from her schooldays and her years at University College and An Taibhdhearc. She felt it was her first real homecoming:

Until now – because I was only able to make brief visits to Galway, I felt a strange, mixed nostalgia – terribly happy walking around the streets, then getting a catch of loneliness for the past when my mother, father and sister were here, too. This time because I'm involved in the play and here for a good while, I've totally settled down.[16]

On one free-day, during the Galway run, she asked Johnny Hippisley to drive her to Rosmuc in Connemara to visit Pearse's cottage. As they walked the rising path by the seashore from the road to the cottage, Johnny noticed that she seemed short of breath. He thought that the physical strain of the part was too much for her. Her son, Donnacha felt that she had aged very quickly. He was happily married in 1980, to an air hostess from Dun Laoghaire, Patricia Cork, and Siobhán was proud of her grandson Eoin, born in 1985 and named after her father, and her granddaughter Aoife, born in 1986.

When she played Mommo for a month with the Druid company at the Donmar Theatre, London, in the spring of 1986, all her old friends and a few of her sternest critics acclaimed the "sheer theatrical magic" of the occasion. A humorous but ominous note was sent backstage signed: "A Fan. A Fan. Richard Harris".

> I was one among the many mesmerised and worshipping at your temple last Wednesday night ... The performance was smooth, delicate, tender and very moving.
>
> You looked exhausted, therefore I did not wish to intrude on what remained of your energy by invading you after the show. With great respect, I quelled my desire to embrace you. I thought, Jesus, she might collapse in me arms and then what would I do? The options are many. You may not have approved.
>
> You were glorious, you are glorious, you will always be glorious ...[17]

Apart from a voice-over for a Beckett film, *Eh Joe*, made by Yellow Asylum Films, her last performance was as Mommo on 24 May 1986, at the end of a fortnight's run of *Bailegangaire* at the Gaiety Theatre, Dublin. The Druid production had transferred admirably from their tiny stage to the Victorian vastness of the Gaiety. I recall vividly Mommo's tortured grimaces which, at times, looked like a Francis Bacon portrait. Siobhán was still able to place her voice in any register, from an animal growl to a high-pitched giggle. Yet behind the cackling senility there was an inner warmth and the innocence of a child.

I never saw her again except briefly when she attended an Abbey Theatre shareholders meeting in September. She came to those frequently routine affairs whenever she was free but seldom spoke, and when she did it was to praise a play or an actor. At the end of Lelia Doolan's term as Artistic Director, she expressed regret at the departure of an old friend. Off the record, she said that Lelia "did not know what she was doing" when she directed an unhappy production of *Saint Joan*. At the end of the 1986 meeting, for no known reason, she came over and shook my hand in silent farewell. Only once had she taken me to task, when she felt that I should have arranged for a funeral oration at the graveside of Ernest Blythe. She may have had her own back when she failed to turn up to say a few words at Frank Dermody's funeral in St Fintan's, Sutton, and I had to stand in for her at the last moment. One of her last plans, according to Tomás MacAnna, was to translate *The Trojan Women* into Irish and to play Hecuba with the Abbey company at the open-air theatre in Agrinion in Greece.[18]

In the autumn of 1986 she complained of a bad cough and chest pains and she had check-ups at Beaumont Hospital. It was not until early November that she told her family and closest friends that she had lung cancer. She was admitted to the Blackrock Clinic, where she was operated on twice owing to complications. A tumour was removed by the leading heart surgeon, Mr Maurice Neligan. The operation was regarded as successful, but she had an unexpected heart attack. She lapsed into a coma and died twelve hours later at 10 a.m. on Sunday 16 November 1986.

The tributes from public figures were instant and sincere. The president, Patrick Hillery, spoke of

> her enrichment of so many aspects of Irish life at home, and the enhancement of Irish life everywhere through her exceptional talents.[19]

An Taoiseach, Dr Garrett Fitzgerald, said:

> The tragic death of Siobhán McKenna has deprived us of a unique talent which commanded the admiration and respect of theatre-goers everywhere. No one who has seen her on stage will forget her presence, her voice, or the range of emotions she could portray and could arouse. She was an outstanding representative of Irish culture outside Ireland, as well as at home, as for example, when she played to the King and Queen of the Belgians during the State visit of President and Mrs Childers a decade ago.[20]

The only comment by a political figure on her work as a member of the Council of State came from the leader of the Opposition, Mr Charles Haughey TD, who said that

> her commitment to the Irish language and culture, both as an actress and a member of the Council of State, was outstanding.[21]

A second leader in *The Irish Times*, concluded:

Happily, she herself retained to the end of her days the humour, grace and generosity of spirit that made her not only admired but much loved by her friends, colleagues and audiences.[22]

It is notoriously more difficult to pay tribute to one who was a rival than to a friend. For that reason, Cyril Cusack's comment is memorable:

Her death must leave a continual pang, in a sense it may be seen as a martyrdom to theatre for, as I know from my experience as her colleague, she suffered in her work, giving of herself completely to the agony as well as the ecstasy of our calling.

Perhaps I should add, typically she took our only professional time-off, a Sunday, to leave us. May I quote from the poet T.S. Eliot, whose words eloquently express what I attempt to say:
As, in a theatre,
The lights are extinguished for the scene to be changed –
So our darkness shall be light,
and the stillness the dancing...
Echoed ecstasy not lost.[23]

At her requiem mass, at the Church of the Three Patrons, Rathgar, the Siamsa Tíre group from Tralee sang Father Pat Ahern's *Aifreann Pádraig Naofa* and Father Dermod McCarthy gave the homily in which he told the packed congregation of Siobhán's last little joke:

We will always remember her wide open eyes, searching, wondering, and then predictably a twinkle, and that deep infectious laugh. Hadn't she a marvellous sense of fun? Only a couple of days ago when she was quite ill and lying in the intensive care unit with the fan blowing beside her bed, her dear friend, Johnny Hippisley said, "I'll put this fan back a bit," and Siobhán quipped, "I didn't think they'd bring the fans in here."[24]

Later that afternoon the people of Galway City stood silent in the rain as her funeral cortège passed the scenes of her childhood, An Taibhdhearc and the old house in Shantalla. The Professor's daughter who never went to an acting class and who was reared far from the hit or miss of the fit-ups, was making her last exit.

Around the graveside of her parents in Rahoon stood her sister Nancy, her son Donnacha, Seán Ó hÓráin, Johnny Hippisley,

Bishop Eamon Casey and, lost among the crowd, all the great characters she had brought to life – San Siobhán, Pegeen Mike, Molly Bloom, Cass Maguire and Mommo – mumbling a final prayer for the living and the dead.

Brian Friel's words of farewell brought a glimmer of brightness through the rain-drenched gloom of that November evening:

"A star," he said, "is an abused and abased word but in the language of the theatre it retained an exact meaning. In theatre, a star was an actress who was unique in that she personified an idea a country has of itself at any particular time. It may not be a definition that bears too close a scrutiny, but when you apply it to someone like Siobhán, you begin to get the feel of its worth. Siobhán was our pre-eminent Irish star, indeed our only star. For people of my generation, she personified an idea of Ireland."[25]

That sixth sense, without which an artist like Brian Friel cannot flourish, seemed to tell us that Siobhán – it always seemed superfluous to add a surname – was the greatest actress we had known. She was in the tradition of those great stage actors who were never directors' puppets and who did not rely on camera angles or the cosmetics of the cutting room to capture a passive audience. Fame and fashion are fickle but there will always be a murmur of Siobhán's greatness in the seashell of memory, the most enduring of the muses. At least, she must share in Louis Untermeyer's tribute to Sara Allgood:

Oh woman, you are magic manifold
You stab the silence with a voice of gold
That throbs with clamorous seas and rolling moors
You speak – and Age forgets that it is old;
The dying moment lives – the hour endures
A deathless echo of immortal lures.[26]

Notes

1. *Die Furche*, 16 May 1979
2. *Kurier*, 9 September 1980
3. Edward L. Shaughnessy, *Eugene O'Neill in Ireland* (Greenwood Press, 1988) p.107
4. Seamus Martin, *Irish Times*, 13 October 1984
5. Fintan O'Toole, *Sunday Tribune*, 14 October 1986

6. W.B. Yeats, introduction to *The Midnight Court*, translated by Percy Arland Ussher (London 1926) pp.11-12
7. Ibid. pp.17-18
8. Joyce McGreevy Stafford, interview with Siobhán McKenna, *Galway Advertiser*, 5 December 1985
9. Ibid.
10. *Sunday Tribune*, 20 December 1985
11. Ibid.
12. Interview with Niall Buggy
13. Translated from the Irish by Kuno Meyer.
14. Fintan O'Toole, "The Old Woman's Brood," *Sunday Tribune*, 8 December 1985
15. Colm Toibín, *Irish Independent*, 8 December 1985
16. Joyce McGreevy Stafford, interview with Siobhán McKenna, *Sunday Independent*, 8 December 1985
17. Extract from note from Richard Harris, quoted in the *Irish Press*, 16 May 1987
18. Tomás MacAnna, unpublished reminiscences, January 1933
19. *Irish Times*, 17 November 1986
20. Ibid.
21. *Irish Times*, 18 November 1986
22. Ibid.
23. An appreciation by Cyril Cusack, op. cit.
24. *Irish Press*, 18 November 1986
25. *Irish Press*, 19 November 1986
26. *Collected Poems of Louis Untermeyer.*

Bibliography

Allt and Alspach (eds) *The Variorum Edition of the Poems of W. B. Yeats*, Macmillan 1957

Arland Ussher, Percy (trans) *The Midnight Court* and *The Adventures of a Luckless Fellow*, London 1926

Fallon, Gabriel, *The Abbey Actor*, Dublin n.d.

Fitzhenry, Edna, *The Nineteen-Sixteen Anthology*, Browne & Nolan 1935

Fitz-Simon, Christopher, *The Boys*, Gill & Macmillan 1994

Gregory, Lady, *Our Irish Theatre*, Putnams 1913

Hay, Peter, *Theatrical Anecdotes*, Oxford University Press 1987

Hickey, Des, and Smith, Gus, *A Paler Shade of Green*, Leslie Frewen 1972

Hogan, Robert, *After the Irish Renaissance*, University of Minnesota Press 1967

Hunt, Hugh, *The Abbey Theatre*, Gill & Macmillan 1979

Joyce, James, *Pomes Penyeach*, Faber & Faber 1966

Krause, David (ed), *Letters of Sean O'Casey*, Vol II, Macmillan n.d.

Lawrence, Dan H. and Laurence, Max, *The Bernard Shaw Collected Letters 1926-1950*, London 1988

Matthews, Aidan Carl (ed), *The Immediate Man*, Dolmen Press 1983

Nic Siúbhlaigh, Máire, *The Splendid Years*, Duffy 1955

Ó hAodha Micheál, *Theatre in Ireland*, Blackwell 1974
Ó hAodha Micheál, *The Importance of Being Micheál: A Portrait of MacLiammóir*, Brandon 1991
Ó Dúlaing, Donncha, *Voices of Ireland*, O'Brien Press/RTE 1985
O'Connor, Ulick, *Brendan Behan: A Biography*, Hamish Hamilton 1970
Payn, G. and Morley, S. (eds), *The Noel Coward Diaries*, London 1982
Pearse, P.H, *Plays, Stories and Poems*, Talbot Press 1963
Pine, Richard, *Brian Friel and Ireland's Drama*, London 1990
Robinson, Lennox, *Ireland's Abbey Theatre*, Sidgwick & Jackson 1951
Shaughnessy, Edward L, *Eugene O'Neill in Ireland*, Greenwood Press 1988
Shaw, G. B., *Saint Joan*, Penguin Books 1964
Shaw, G. B., *Dramatic Opinions and Essays*, Constable 1907
Stephens, James, *Collected Poems*, Macmillan 1926
Tynan, Kenneth, *Curtains*, Longman, London 1961
Williams, Kenneth, *The Kenneth Williams Diaries*, HarperCollins 1993
Yeats, W. B. (ed), *Samhain*, Maunsel 1904
Young, Jordan R, *The Beckett Actor*, Moonstone Press 1987

Index

185